TWIST

Your Guide to Creating Inspired Craft Cocktails

JORDAN HUGHES

Creator of High-Proof Preacher

PAGE STREET
PUBLISHING CO.

PAGE STREET
PUBLISHING CO.

First published in 2022 by
Page Street Publishing Co.
27 Congress Street, Suite 1511
Salem, MA 01970
www.pagestreetpublishing.com

Distributed by Macmillan, sales in Canada by The Canadian Manda Group.

26 25   24   23   22   1 2   3 4 5

ISBN-13: 978-1-64567-648-5
ISBN-10: 1-64567-648-X

Library of Congress Control Number: 2022940200

Cover and book design by Emma Hardy for Page Street Publishing Co.
Photography by Jordan Hughes

Printed and bound in the United States of America

To all the skilled bartenders I have had the pleasure of
sitting across the bar from—thank you for doing what
you do and for inspiring so much creativity
and hospitality.

TABLE OF CONTENTS

PDX   H   USA

CLASSIC COCKTAILS AS TEMPLATES

There's a reason that we call drinks like the Old Fashioned (page 52), Martini (page 64) and Margarita (page 39) "classics." These cocktail recipes have stood the test of time. Just like music or fashion, cocktail trends come and go, falling in and out of style, but there are certain classic cocktails that have stuck around through it all. Most of these classics are incredibly simple and contain very minimal ingredients. Take the Daiquiri (page 27), for example. Although it's been bastardized by cruise lines and big box restaurant chains in recent decades, a truly classic daiquiri is only rum, lime juice and Simple Syrup (page 160)—and it's simply incredible.

Remembering the first few "original" cocktail recipes I came up with is both frustrating and hilarious. I was enamored with the endless possiblities and combined ingredients I thought sounded good, like tequila, lemon juice and honey. Why not add some fresh ginger too? So, I put those four things in a shaker and poured it up. There was nothing out there or over-the-top about the drink. It was intuitive . . . but also pretty terrible.

When it comes to making quality cocktails there is still an art form involved (or is it science, or combination of both?). It involves more than combining complementary flavors in a shaker. It takes knowledge of the ingredients and executing the proper techniques to craft a truly exceptional mixed drink.

Although I was eager to untether myself from classic cocktail recipes, it was through mastering them that I was able to unlock the vast world of mixology. Using the Daiquiri as an example once again, it is made up of a strong spirit (rum), a sour element (lime juice) and a bit of sweetness to balance it out (Simple Syrup). Let's say you want to use tequila in place of rum. Well now, you essentially have a Margarita: a completely different drink, although it follows the same building blocks as the Daiquiri (strong, sour, sweet). It almost seems too easy, but this is where we start getting creative. I understand the urge to want to start tossing random ingredients from your fridge into your shaker and seeing what comes out, but try and resist the temptation. The best cocktails are often subtle and simple, and we can learn the most from basic recipes. There is no need to reinvent the wheel. The classics are classic for a reason and are essentially your templates for cocktail creation. But once you know the classics you can always build on them, mold them . . . or give them a special *twist*.

BAR BASICS: GETTING STARTED

Getting started with making cocktails and stocking your home bar can be daunting. As a perfectionist, I generally don't bother doing anything unless I can do it really well. When it came to getting started with making cocktails, I felt like I needed to go out and buy all the best barware and get all the necessary bottles to make every drink all at once (if that's even possible). But if you're like me, you're not made of money and mixology isn't exactly an inexpensive pursuit. It's important to realize that you may never be able to make "every drink." Even after years and years of learning, collecting and expanding my liquor cabinet, I still often come across drink recipes that contain one or several ingredients I don't have. Although it's a frustrating idea, just let go of the notion that you need to buy every ingredient and tool imaginable to make cocktails.

Instead, think through some cocktails that you enjoy drinking—and maybe some that you'll likely make for others—and start by only purchasing the tools and ingredients you need to make those specific cocktails. One example: Are you a Margarita (page 39) fan? Pick up some good tequila, orange liqueur and stock some fresh limes in the fridge. Then for bar tools, get yourself a cocktail shaker, a strainer, a jigger for measuring and a hand-juicer for juicing the limes. Just stick with those few things for now and then you can build on them later. You can get different varieties of tequila or experiment with different salt or spicy rims. Basically, become really good at making Margaritas and expand on your skills and ingredients when you feel ready. I find this approach a lot more realistic and attainable than buying up a bunch of tools or ingredients that you may never use.

All that said, stocking a home bar is personal, and although I'm happy to share my own recommendations with you, there are likely things that I enjoy and consider "essential" that you won't. There are a lot of recommendations in the following pages, from barware and glassware to spirits and various other cocktail ingredients. If you were to go out and buy everything at once you would likely have a pretty well-rounded bar set-up. But again, try to release yourself from that pressure of needing to have "everything." As you start making drinks for yourself and for others, you'll get a better sense of what tools you need and what ingredients you use the most.

ESSENTIAL BAR TOOLS

Shaker

Quite possibly the most ubiquitous bar tool, there are various shaker designs to choose from, three-piece Cobbler shaker being the one you're most likely already familiar with. Most professionals prefer something called a Boston shaker or a tin-on-tin shaker, as these designs are better suited for fast-paced bar environments. Don't have a shaker? You can use a mason jar and a screw-on lid instead.

Mixing Glass

These elegant vessels are typically wide-based containers made from glass with a pour spout and beautiful designs and patterns etched into them. A mixing glass is intended for making stirred cocktails, as the wide base allows for more surface contact with the ice and its seamless design allows you to stir with a controlled, continuous motion. Don't have a mixing glass? You can use a French press.

Jigger

This small bar tool is absolutely essential for making accurate measurements and consistent cocktails again and again. Alternately, you could use a shot glass for measuring, but generally jiggers are more ergonomic and have multiple markers on them for different measurements.

Strainer(s)

This tool is used after shaking or stirring your cocktail when you are ready to pour it into a glass. The purpose of the strainer is to hold back the ice and/or any other ingredients used for mixing the cocktail that you don't want in your finished drink. A Hawthorne strainer is made with a tightly wound spring that allows the user to push down on a metal tab and adjust the level of strain while pouring. A julep strainer is a bit more old-fashioned, essentially just a large spoon with small holes in it. You could also benefit from a conical mesh strainer, which are often used with Hawthorne strainers, to help filter out small particles like small ice chips or herbs.

Barspoon

Barspoons have various uses from being the ideal tool for stirring spirit-forward cocktails, to allowing the user to pour carbonated beverages down their spiral shafts into a glass without the beverage bubbling over (thus their spiral design). Avoid inexpensive barspoons with rubber red tips on one end. These tend to bend and break easily.

Citrus Juicer

When making drinks, you'll likely be using a lot of fresh citrus. Save your hands by getting a citrus hand juicer. They're easy to find and inexpensive, and you'll get a lot of use out of it.

ESSENTIAL SPIRITS & INGREDIENTS

As mentioned previously, stocking a home bar is personal, so you should buy bottles and ingredients that you enjoy drinking and using. If you're new to making cocktails yourself, this will take some time to figure out, so start small. As you start making more cocktails and sampling more spirits, you'll get a better understanding of what you like. As you go through the recipes in this book, I will suggest various products that I personally recommend for each cocktail so you have guidance along the way. But of course, I understand the desire to have a well-rounded home bar; something that has most of the bases covered and can accommodate a variety of drink requests. And hey, I appreciate a good list, so here's my own list of essential spirits, liqueurs and other ingredients that are helpful to have on hand.

BASE SPIRITS

Whiskey

There is a wide variety of whiskey you can choose from. I'd start with one bottle of bourbon and one bottle of rye whiskey. A good starting point would be Buffalo Trace Bourbon and Rittenhouse Rye. Bourbon is made primarily of corn, so it tends to be more sweet. Rye is, unsurprisingly made from rye and is characterized by having a distinctive spice to it. Eventually, add a bottle from both Ireland and Scotland, like Slane Irish Whiskey and Famous Grouse Blended Scotch. Single malt scotch tends to be more expensive, but does have some uses in mixed drinks as well.

Gin

There is a wide variety of styles and flavors to discover with gin, so don't get too comfortable with one type. Start with some standard issue London-dry gins for cocktails, like Beefeater Gin (inexpensive and easy to find) or Bombay Sapphire (another standard issue London-dry). London-dry gins are very juniper-forward, which is the defining botanical in gin, but there are other styles that range from citrus to floral, to even savory. Once you're comfortable with the basics, branch out into different styles to fully explore all that gin has to offer.

Vodka

To be honest, I don't use vodka often, but it's good to have on hand. Reyka Vodka is my personal go-to. It's a good "blank canvas" if you want other ingredients to take center stage in your cocktail. However, in the words of bar veteran, former chef and author Sother Teague, "Given the options, I'd never start a soup with water. I'd always choose a stock of some kind. The same principle applies to drink making."

Tequila

Do some research here and pick up a couple bottles of high-quality, 100% blue agave tequila. You can start by getting one tequila blanco (meaning white or unaged) and a tequila reposado, which has been rested in barrels for several months and is a bit more "mellow" in flavor from aging. Pueblo Viejo is an affordable brand that is widely available in many regions and comes highly recommended from many bartenders. Also be sure to explore some mezcal. It is a diverse category, with unique terroir-driven flavor profiles depending on the region and agave used. Anything by Banhez Mezcal is highly recommended, as well as Del Maguey.

Rum

Yet another spirit category that is incredibly diverse (maybe the most diverse of all) is rum. Every rum producing region has their own rules and traditions, so rum will taste different depending on the production methods used and the region of origin. Unfortunately, the color of the rum (like white or gold) is not an accurate indicator of what it will taste like. There is also a lot of very low-quality and outright bad rum lining the shelves of many liquor stores. Personally, I lean toward Jamaican rums for their unique and funky flavor profiles. Some bottles and brands to keep an eye out for are Smith & Cross, Flor de Caña, Probitas and Hampden Estate.

Brandy

Brandy is distilled from grapes or other fruits (like apples or pears). Brandy can have a broad range of flavor profiles and aromas, ranging from fruity and floral, to dark with rich notes of cinnamon and oak. Cognac is a form of brandy that is made specifically in the Cognac region of France and is aged in oak. Consider picking up a bottle of cognac and a bottle of aged brandy from another region of the world to compare. Some of my favorite cognacs come from the French brand Rémy Martin. Then, try an American brandy from Copper & Kings.

Miscellaneous Base Spirits

There are plenty of other base spirits to consider, but some of my favorites are pisco, aquavit and absinthe. Pisco is another form of brandy from South America. It tends to be semi-sweet with distinctive grape notes balanced by herbal elements. Aquavit is a grain spirit flavored with various Scandinavian botanicals, like star anise and caraway, often giving it a savory flavor. Absinthe has a colorful history that deserves its own book, but it is an incredibly unique and flavorful French spirit that many compare flavor-wise to black licorice.

MODIFIERS

Liqueurs

A liqueur is a spirit that has been sweetened or has additional flavoring from fruits, herbs or spices. Liqueurs can be enjoyed on their own (usually as a form of dessert) or used as the sweetening element in a cocktail. Some liqueurs are very sweet, while others are drier and some are floral. Others can be bitter and savory such as amari, which is a broad category of bittersweet liqueurs mainly from Italy.

There's a lot to unpack in the world of liqueurs, but for your home bar, I recommend having some dry curaçao or triple sec, some popular Italian bitter liqueurs like Campari and Aperol and green and yellow Chartreuse from France.

Fortified Wines

This includes things like vermouth and sherry, both of which play a strong "supporting role" in many spirit-forward cocktails. To start out, I recommend having at least one bottle of dry vermouth and one bottle of sweet vermouth. Sherry isn't as essential to keep around, but I tend to have some amontillado sherry on hand. Even though they are fortified wines, keep in mind that they do not last forever. Over time, they may start to oxidize and begin to taste like vinegar, which isn't necessarily bad, but it's not usually something you want in your cocktail.

Bitters

When it comes to making cocktails, bitters are like your spices. They are typically added to drinks in small amounts or "dashes." If used well, you likely won't notice them but, similar to eating an unseasoned dish, you'll notice when bitters are absent. Most bitters are highly concentrated (with a high alcohol content on their own) which is why they are used sparingly. Aromatic bitters are commonly used in a variety of cocktails and are widely available at most liquor stores. However, I'd recommend the "trinity" of cocktail bitters: aromatic bitters, as well as orange bitters and a third called Peychaud's bitters, which is a bit sweeter than aromatic bitters with flavors of cherry and anise.

Syrups

Using sugar syrup in cocktails not only helps with the overall balance of flavors, but it also adds texture, like cooking with butter. Syrup, when used properly and in moderation, helps bind certain ingredients together and provides a smooth, less harsh mouthful. The most common cocktail syrup is Simple Syrup (page 160), which is made by combing equal parts sugar and water (very simple). However, I also recommend having some rich Demerara Syrup (page 160) on hand, especially for using in cocktails with aged spirits.

Fresh Fruit & Herbs

It's hard to keep fresh ingredients stocked due to their short shelf life, but I make it a habit to pick up several fresh limes, lemons and oranges if I plan on making cocktails that week. Using fresh citrus in cocktails is so much better than using pre-bottled sour mix or other store-bought juices that tend to be full of preservatives and added sugar. When it comes to ingredients like herbs, this obviously involves some planning depending on what you'll be making that week. Better yet, consider starting a small herb garden at home so you can have a steady supply of mint, rosemary, thyme or anything else you may want to incorporate into your drinks.

Ice

After you've spent all this time and money on making fancy cocktails, the last thing you want to do is use low-quality ice. I typically avoid those foggy, half-moons that your freezer door makes, as they tend to have an odd, chemical taste to them. Ice does easily absorb other flavors, so keep this in mind when you're making it and place your ice molds on a separate shelf from any food. You can pick up silicon molds that make large, square cubes that are ideal for shaking, stirring and serving as well as long ice spear molds that are used for drinks served in tall glasses like the Highball (page 86). You can make your own cracked ice by breaking off pieces of regular ice, or crushed ice by hitting regular cubes with a mallet. Both kinds cool drinks at a more rapid pace and are often used in Tiki cocktails to keep them chilled.

IMPORTANT TECHNIQUES & TERMS

Shake
This involves combing the necessary cocktail ingredients in a metal tin and shaking vigorously with ice. This process not only mixes the ingredients together, but also rapidly chills them and adds dilution as the ice melts. As a general rule of thumb, shake cocktails that contain citrus, egg white or cream.

Stir
This technique involves stirring the necessary cocktail ingredients in a glass mixing vessel. This process is gentler than shaking, allowing you to have more control over dilution and the final texture of your cocktail. Generally, cocktails are to be stirred when they are made primarily with clear ingredients that are easily integrated together, like most spirit-forward cocktails.

Double-Strain or Fine-Strain
This refers to using a fine-mesh strainer (or tea strainer) in addition to a standard Hawthorne strainer when pouring your cocktail. This method is typically used when serving a shaken cocktail that is served up (without ice), as the mesh strainer prevents any small ice shards from ending up in the final drink.

Dry Shake
This technique involves shaking a cocktail without ice first, then shaking again with ice added to the shaker. A dry shake is typically used when making drinks that have egg white in them.

Float
This refers to adding another ingredient (often a spirit or syrup) to the top of a finished cocktail. These Ingredients are typically carefully poured over the back of a barspoon to allow them to float on top of the drink more easily.

Rinse
This involves coating a glass with a specific ingredient (often a strong, aromatic spirit like absinthe) before a cocktail is poured into it. It is done by pouring a small amount of the ingredient into the glass, swirling it around, then discarding.

Serve Up
This term is used to describe serving a finished drink without ice, typically in a stemmed glass like a coupe.

Serve Neat
This term is used to describe serving a spirit on its own, un-chilled and without ice.

Rocks
This term simply means to serve over ice.

SHAKEN COCKTAILS

The cocktail shaker is quite possibly the most ubiquitous and easily recognizable bar tool in existence. It's an essential piece of equipment for every bartender and cocktail enthusiast alike, as it's used for making a whole gamut of popular drinks from Whiskey Sours (page 20) and Margaritas (page 39) to the notorious Ramos Gin Fizz (page 109).

A common question is how do you know when to shake a cocktail (versus stirring it)? While there are always exceptions to this guideline, the general rule of thumb is that if a cocktail contains any sort of thick or foggy ingredients (i.e., citrus, cream, egg white, etc.) it should be shaken with ice. These types of ingredients need more kinetic energy in order to be broken down and incorporated into the other ingredients.

Shaking a cocktail does several things. It rapidly chills the mixture by essentially "throwing" pieces of ice back and forth rapidly within your shaker. These chunks of ice start to break down and will chill the cocktail being made, while simultaneously diluting it. Although "diluting" may sound negative, this is actually an essential process for both balancing your cocktail and achieving the right texture. However, proper care and attention should be taken so as to not overshake or overdilute your cocktail (which used to be referred to as "bruising" a drink).

For most shaken cocktail recipes, fill your shaker with ice until the level of ice is well above the level of liquid in your shaker. Close the shaker and shake hard for roughly 15 seconds, or until your hands start to get cold. The exact timing will vary depending on the quality of ice you use. For example, inexpensive pellet ice (the kind you get from a grocery store) will break down and melt quickly, so you'll want to shake briefly. As you shake, you'll notice your shaker will form a layer of "frost" on the outside, which is a good indication that your cocktail is nearly ready to be strained and served.

WHISKEY SOUR

The classic sour consists of spirit, citrus and sugar as its defining components. It's a simple format for cocktail making, but one that has plenty of variance and room for experimentation. The sour is the three-ingredient template that is the backbone for a long list of popular cocktails (many of which are included in this book), but perhaps the most well-known and defining recipe in the category is the Whiskey Sour. This simple drink, consisting of only whiskey, lemon and sugar, has been ubiquitous in taverns, restaurants and bars across America (and beyond) for well over 100 years and has since inspired countless riffs and variations.

For those looking to better understand cocktails and learn how to create their own recipes, I always recommend starting with the Whiskey Sour. At first glance, it's an easy recipe but it's also an incredibly important lesson in how to properly balance cocktails. Even adding as much as ¼ ounce (8 ml) more of lemon juice will shift the flavor profile to be drier or tart. Similarly, adding just a bit more of Simple Syrup (page 160) will often make it too sweet. It's all about dialing in the right ratio of spirit, citrus and sugar to achieve a balanced and delicious flavor profile. Most Whiskey Sours also incorporate raw egg white into the mix to give the drink a velvety foam. This simply adds texture to the drink and doesn't impart any flavor. However, some imbibers might be put off by the idea of raw egg in their beverage. Since you're mixing the egg white with high-proof alcohol, this will likely take care of anything that could upset your stomach, but if you'd rather leave out the egg white, that's totally fine as well.

2 oz (60 ml) bourbon

¾ oz (22 ml) fresh lemon juice

¾ oz (22 ml) Simple Syrup (page 160)

Egg white (optional)

Garnish: maraschino cherry

Combine the bourbon, fresh lemon juice, Simple Syrup and egg white (if using) in a cocktail shaker, and then shake well without ice to help break down and integrate the egg white (this is referred to as "dry shaking"). Open the shaker and add ice, and then shake again. Double-strain into a coupe glass and serve up. Garnish with a maraschino cherry on a cocktail pick.

THE BARTENDER SUGGESTS

Elijah Craig Small Batch Bourbon
Buffalo Trace Bourbon
Luxardo Maraschino Cherries

AMARETTO SOUR

RECIPE BY JEFFREY MORGENTHALER

The Amaretto Sour is a well-known, albeit somewhat reviled, drink in the cocktail world that originated sometime in the 1970s. The disco era is considered somewhat of the "dark ages" for mixology, as most cocktails to come out of that time were largely made with cheap, sugary mixes and were generally just horribly unbalanced and uninspiring. The Amaretto Sour essentially became an archetype for bad cocktails as bartenders in the early 2000s began championing the use of fresh citrus and house-made ingredients. However, thanks to Portland, Oregon, bartender and author, Jeffrey Morgenthaler, the Amaretto Sour has had an incredible resurgence in popularity. Morgenthaler has a knack for chasing away the pretentious nature that is sometimes associated with craft cocktail culture and mixology. One such example is how he took this once laughable recipe, made some subtle tweaks to its structure, and made a truly delicious and well-balanced beverage worthy of a spot on any cocktail menu.

The issue with the *original* Amaretto Sour was that it had no backbone. The base spirit (if you can call it that) was just amaretto, a sweet, almond-flavored liqueur mixed with bottled sour mix. It was cloying and unbalanced, and honestly not very pleasant to drink. Morgenthaler adjusted the recipe by adding egg white (bringing a velvety texture to the drink) and fresh lemon juice instead of sour mix. He also added cask-strength bourbon to the mix, punching up the alcohol content and giving the drink that much-needed backbone to balance out the sweetness from the amaretto liqueur. It was a simple but brilliant twist. Nowadays, if you see an Amaretto Sour on a cocktail menu, it is most likely Jeff Morgenthaler's recipe—and it's most definitely worth getting.

1½ oz (45 ml) amaretto

¾ oz (22 ml) cask-proof bourbon

1 oz (30 ml) fresh lemon juice

1 tsp Rich Simple Syrup (page 160)

1 egg white

Garnish: lemon twist and a maraschino cherry

Combine the amaretto, cask-proof bourbon, fresh lemon juice, Rich Simple Syrup and egg white in a cocktail shaker and dry shake. Add ice and shake again. Strain into a rocks glass over fresh ice and garnish with a lemon twist and a maraschino cherry.

THE BARTENDER SUGGESTS

Luxardo Amaretto
Elijah Craig Barrel Proof Bourbon
Old Forester 1920 Prohibition Style Bourbon

MODERN MEDICINE

Here's an original cocktail recipe in the Whiskey Sour (page 20) family. But, as you will soon see throughout this book, most "original recipes" really are riffs on classics, or even riffs on other riffs, as this recipe is somewhat like a modern classic called a Penicillin.

I first made this recipe while visiting a group of friends out of state, and I only had a small selection of liquor bottles I brought with me for making drinks for everyone. Since Whiskey Sours are easy and always a hit, I decided to go that direction in terms of recipe format, but still wanted to change it up slightly and make something that felt more unique.

Although the velvety texture from shaken egg white is nice at times, I personally prefer my Whiskey Sours without it. However, once I mixed up this drink, it did feel like it was missing an element for the recipe to really stand on its own. I reached for a bottle of Laphroaig—a scotch from the region of Islay, which is known for its unmistakably smoky flavor profile—and I carefully floated a bit on top of the finished drink. This method of "floating" another spirit is used in various sour variations, like the New York Sour or the previously mentioned Penicillin (which also uses an Islay scotch float). I hoped this approach would work well and it certainly did!

1½ oz (45 ml) bourbon

½ oz (15 ml) Aperol

¾ oz (22 ml) fresh lemon juice

½ oz (15 ml) Demerara Syrup (page 160)

2 dashes of aromatic bitters

¼ oz (8 ml) smoky scotch

Garnish: lemon twist

Combine the bourbon, Aperol, fresh lemon juice, Demerara Syrup and bitters in a cocktail shaker and shake with ice. Strain into a rocks glass over ice. Carefully float the scotch over the top of the cocktail by slowly pouring it over the back of a barspoon. Then, take a lemon twist and place it on the side of the rim of the glass.

THE BARTENDER SUGGESTS
Russell's Reserve Bourbon
Angostura Aromatic Bitters
Laphroaig 10 Year Islay Scotch

DAIQUIRI

If someone suggests that you get a Daiquiri, what first comes to mind? Unfortunately for many, you might think of a sugary "boat drink" that you'd typically be served on a cruise ship—made with artificial fruits and colors, and maybe even served from a slushie machine in a plastic hurricane glass. I'll admit, sometimes that kind of drink hits the spot on a warm summer vacation but calling it a quality cocktail would feel like quite a stretch. Well, it turns out that a truly classic Daiquiri is a much simpler affair that calls for only three ingredients. All you need is quality rum, fresh lime juice and a bit of sugar syrup, and when combined in the right proportion, it's a magical combination.

Similar to what I described about the Whiskey Sour (page 20), just a slight variation in ingredients (i.e. adding or subtracting ¼ ounce [8 ml]) could shift the balance of this drink toward too sweet or too sour. The balance of flavors also greatly depends on the rum used. Rum is a notoriously unruly spirit, where every country and region that produces the spirit has different regulations about how it can be made (or almost no regulations at all). Many rums are full of additives, like additional sugar that has been added post-distillation. Some rums add a lot of additional sweetness to the cocktail, requiring less sugar syrup to balance the tart element. There are also just drastically different flavor profiles from rum to rum. Some of my favorite rums are from Jamaica or Haiti, which tend to both be described as "funky" because of their unique and very potent flavors of fermented fruit. I also really enjoy using Rhum Agricole in Daiquiris—a style of rum produced from fermented sugar cane juice vs. most rum, which is largely produced from molasses.

All that to say, even though this is an incredibly simple cocktail, there is really so much variety to explore. For a twist, you can keep all the measurements the same and simply swap out the style or brand of rum and you'll experience a completely different flavor profile. Feel free to experiment with the ratio of each ingredient to find the balance that you most enjoy.

2 oz (60 ml) rum

¾ oz (22 ml) fresh lime juice

¾ oz (22 ml) Simple Syrup (page 160)

Combine the rum, fresh lime juice and Simple Syrup in a cocktail shaker and shake with ice. Double-strain into a chilled coupe or Nick & Nora glass and serve up.

THE BARTENDER SUGGESTS

Copalli White Rum
Probitas White Blended Rum

RUM CLUB DAIQUIRI

RECIPE BY KEVIN LUDWIG

This recipe is the house Daiquiri (page 27) at Rum Club in Portland, Oregon, one of my favorite cocktail spots, and this recipe is one of my favorite daiquiris. Rum Club is often referred to as an "industry bar" because it's where a lot of bartenders go to drink on their nights off. It's always busy, but it has an incredibly friendly and approachable atmosphere, thanks to their always welcoming bar team.

Take a closer look at the Rum Club Daiquiri specs below and you'll notice, despite an apparent longer list of ingredients, they follow the daiquiri template very closely. They just change up a few of the main ingredients. They use an aged rum and a Demerara Syrup (page 160) for balance, which is made from a darker sugar with added richness that pairs well with aged spirits. They also cut down on the syrup and add in a touch of maraschino liqueur, as well as a few dashes of bitters and Herbsaint (an herbal liqueur similar to absinthe). It's still a daiquiri, but it's also very much their own twist on a classic.

2 oz (60 ml) aged rum

¾ oz (22 ml) fresh lime juice

½ oz (15 ml) Demerara Syrup (page 160)

¼ oz (8 ml) maraschino liqueur

2 dashes aromatic bitters

3–5 drops of Herbsaint or absinthe

Combine the aged rum, fresh lime juice, Demerara Syrup, maraschino liqueur, bitters and Herbsaint in a cocktail shaker and shake with ice. Double-strain into a chilled coupe and serve up.

THE BARTENDER SUGGESTS

Flor de Caña 7 Gran Reserva Rum
Plantation Original Dark Rum
Maraska Maraschino
Herbsaint Original 100 Proof

GUAVA DAIQUIRI

The Guava Daiquiri can be made simply by swapping out the cane sugar syrup from a classic Daiquiri (page 27) with guava syrup. Guavas aren't always easy to find in your local grocery store (depending on where you live), but there are some premade guava syrup options you can purchase fairly easily.

For my Guava Daiquiri, I make a few other small changes to the standard recipe by suggesting the use of clairin—an incredibly "funky" and vegetal rum that packs a ton of flavor on its own. At the time of writing, clairin isn't as widely available in every market just yet, but it is certainly gaining a lot of popularity amongst bartenders. If you can't find any clairin, I'd suggest using Rhum Agricole as the next closest substitute. This recipe also includes a few sprays of absinthe over the surface of the finished drink from a small spray bottle. Absinthe carries a lot of myth and mystery (and misinformation) in pop culture, but it's also a really amazing and flavorful spirit. It can be overpowering, so using it in small amounts, such as in dashes or sprays, is best for giving your cocktail a subtle but flavorful upgrade. The taste of absinthe is often compared to black licorice because of its anise component, but when adding to cocktails, it's almost like using salt when cooking: It tends to elevate and compliment flavors that you otherwise wouldn't have noticed.

2 oz (60 ml) Haitian rhum

1 oz (30 ml) fresh lime juice

¾ oz (22 ml) guava syrup

Spritz of absinthe

Garnish: lime wheel

Combine Haitian rhum, fresh lime juice and guava syrup in a cocktail shaker and shake with ice. Strain into a rocks glass over crushed or pebble ice. Garnish by placing a lime wheel next to the rim of the glass. Using an atomizer, add one or two sprays of absinthe to the surface of the cocktail.

THE BARTENDER SUGGESTS

Clairin Vaval Haitian Rum
Rhum Clement Premiere Canne
Reál Guava Syrup
St. George Absinthe Verte

SIDECAR

The Sidecar is a classic cocktail most often served with cognac or brandy, but it's yet another cocktail format where it's easy to change out the base spirit (try it with bourbon or an aged tequila). It's very similar to the sour cocktail format—spirit, citrus and sugar syrup. But as a sour calls for sugar syrup for balance, the Sidecar uses orange liqueur, either on its own or in conjunction with Simple Syrup (page 160). Although simple in appearance, it's a cocktail that can be difficult to get right. The right balance of flavor really does depend on the freshness of citrus used, as well as which orange liqueur and base spirit.

In pre-prohibition days, the Sidecar was served with a sugar-crusted rim. Although some bartenders still insist on it, serving a sidecar this way has largely fallen out of fashion. Personally, I feel that the sugared rim distracts from the delicate balance of this cocktail so instead, I prefer to add just a teaspoon of Rich Simple Syrup (page 160) into this typically three-ingredient cocktail. In this case, the syrup helps to bind the drink's various ingredients together and adds just the right amount of texture without masking its delicate flavors.

1½ oz (45 ml) cognac

¾ oz (22 ml) fresh lemon juice

¾ oz (22 ml) quality orange liqueur

1 tsp Rich Simple Syrup (page 160)

Garnish: orange peel

Combine the cognac, fresh lemon juice, orange liqueur and Rich Simple Syrup in a cocktail shaker and shake with ice. Double-strain into a Nick & Nora glass and serve up. Garnish by delicately placing an orange peel on the rim of the glass.

THE BARTENDER SUGGESTS

Martell VS Cognac
Pierre Ferrand 1840 Cognac
Pierre Ferrand Dry Curaçao

BANANA SIDECAR

Here's an original twist on a Sidecar (page 32) that is always a fun way to impress your friends. A lot of cognacs naturally have a subtle banana-like flavor to them, so swapping out the orange liqueur for banana liqueur was an easy switch. I'm certainly not the first person to make the cognac and banana pairing, but it's a fun combination to play with. For this specific cocktail, a slightly older cognac that has spent more time in a barrel does really well here, as there's usually more vanilla and baking spice notes present (see The Bartender Suggests below).

The fun part (besides drinking it) is definitely the garnish. Garnishes should generally be simple, understated and make sense for that cocktail, but every now and then, you might as well color outside the lines. So, for the Banana Sidecar, I serve it with a small snack: a brûléed banana slice on a cocktail pick (instructions below). It involves using a culinary torch; so I like to bring the drink out to the guest I'm serving it to, set it down on the table but ask them to wait before taking a sip. Then, I make the garnish in front of them by dipping it in sugar and torching it as my guests "ooh and ahh."

1½ oz (45 ml) cognac

¾ oz (22 ml) fresh lemon juice

½ oz (15 ml) banana liqueur

¼ oz (8 ml) Demerara Syrup (page 160)

3 dashes tropical spice bitters

Spritz of Jamaican rum

1 banana slice, for garnish

Pinch of demerara sugar, for garnish

Garnish: brûléed banana slice

Combine the cognac, fresh lemon juice, banana liqueur, Demerara Syrup and bitters in a cocktail shaker and shake with ice. Double-strain into a chilled coupe and serve up. Using an atomizer, add a spray of Jamaican rum to the surface.

For the garnish, take a small slice of banana and put it on a cocktail pick. Tap one side of the banana slice in Demerara sugar (it should naturally stick to the banana slice). Small drips of caramelized sugar will likely drip into your cocktail (which can throw off the flavor balance) so be careful here and try not to add too much sugar to the garnish. Using a culinary torch, briefly torch the sugar-crusted banana slice until the sugar caramelizes. Then, balance the garnish on the rim of the cocktail.

THE BARTENDER SUGGESTS

Rémy Martin 1738 Accord Royal Cognac
Pierre Ferrand Dry Curaçao
Bittermens Elemakule Tiki Bitters

SINGANI CRUSTA

This drink is actually a simple twist on another classic cocktail that is closely related to the Sidecar (page 32): the Brandy Crusta. It has a very similar structure with a cognac base and it relies on the freshest lemon juice and top-shelf orange liqueur for balance. The biggest differentiator for the Brandy Crusta from the Sidecar really is the garnish: a sugar-encrusted rim with a "horse's tale," which is a long spiral of lemon peel that wraps into a circle and balances perfectly behind the rim of the glass. It doesn't sound like much (especially since a Sidecar *used to have* the sugared rim as well) but a Brandy Crusta *without* this signature garnish placed in just such a way is not a Brandy Crusta at all.

Really, my only twist to this recipe is swapping out the cognac (a form of brandy) for singani, which is brandy from Bolivia. It is a fairly significant change to the overall flavor profile of the Brandy Crusta, as singani is much more floral and perfumy. Singani is often compared to pisco, as they are both clear spirits distilled from grapes, and they do share a lot of similar characteristics. This Bolivian spirit has been growing greatly in popularity among bartenders, so definitely keep an eye out for a bottle.

2 oz (60 ml) singani

½ oz (15 ml) orange curaçao

½ oz (15 ml) fresh lemon juice

¼ oz (8 ml) Rich Simple Syrup (page 160)

2 dashes aromatic bitters

Garnish: lemon peel and sugar rim

Prepare a coupe by rimming the glass with a lemon wedge and gently dipping the rim in sugar. Place the prepared glass in the freezer to chill. Combine the singani, orange curaçao, fresh lemon juice, Rich Simple Syrup and bitters in a shaker and shake with ice. Double-strain into your prepared coupe and serve up. Garnish by taking a lemon and a citrus peeler, carefully peeling the whole lemon in one long, continuous spiral. Carefully place this long swirl of lemon inside the glass, tucked just inside the rim.

THE BARTENDER SUGGESTS
Singani 63
Rujero Singani
Pierre Ferrand Dry Curaçao

MARGARITA

Want to know the cocktail that I make the most often at home (both for myself and guests)? Well this is it: a Margarita. There's truly something special with this combo of quality tequila, fresh lime and a little sugar for balance, along with a flaky sea salt rim. Whether it's a hot summer day or a dark and rainy evening, a good Margarita always hits the spot for me.

If you're going through the recipes in this book chronologically, you'll likely recognize some similar recipe formats. When it comes to their base ingredients, a Margarita and a Daiquiri (page 27) are nearly identical cocktails; one being served with tequila and the other with rum. Yet this one ingredient difference makes them clearly two different cocktails. This recipe may also remind you of our Sidecar (page 32), relying on ¾ ounce (22 ml) of a top-shelf orange liqueur and just a scant ¼ ounce (8 ml) of sugar syrup for balance (I use Agave Simple Syrup [page 161] here because it is being paired with tequila, which is an agave spirit). If you'd rather keep things simple, you can also make a great Margarita without the orange liqueur, and just up the Agave Syrup to ½ ounce (15 ml) or ¾ ounce (22 ml) depending on your preference. You can also sub out the Agave Syrup for other syrups to create different flavors. I recommend trying it with Fresh Watermelon Syrup (page 164).

2 oz (60 ml) tequila

¾ oz (22 ml) orange liqueur

1 oz (30 ml) fresh lime juice

¼ oz (8 ml) Agave Simple Syrup (page 161)

Garnish: coarse sea salt rim and a lime wheel

Take a slice of lime and rim the edge of a rocks glass. Then rub the edge of the glass in flaky sea salt and set aside. Combine the tequila, orange liqueur, fresh lime juice and Agave Simple Syrup in a shaker and shake with ice. Strain over fresh ice in your prepared rocks glass and garnish with a lime wheel by placing it directly in the glass.

THE BARTENDER SUGGESTS

Tequila Fortaleza Blanco
La Gritona Reposado (A bit mellower than blanco, with flavors of vanilla and oak from aging)
Cointreau

SPICY MANGO MARGARITA

This twist on a Margarita (page 39) was inspired by one of my favorite treats that I enjoyed while visiting Mexico. A handful of vendors push their carts around on the sandy beaches of Ensenada and offer refreshments to tourists basking in the warm Baja sun. The one that got my attention during my last visit was selling ripe, peeled mangos that were dusted in cayenne pepper and served on a stick like a popsicle. At that moment in time, nothing else could have tasted so incredibly perfect.

This cocktail uses mango puree, which is easy to make at home with a good blender, provided that you can get ahold of some ripe mangos. Simply peel and cut up a mango and add it to a blender with approximately 4 to 5 ounces (120 to 150 ml) of water. Blend and add more water as needed until it reaches your desired consistency. Because of the puree, the cocktail has a much thicker texture than a typical Margarita, making it almost like a fruit smoothie. But if you prefer it to be less thick, simply add more water as you make the puree. Although I serve it up, I do not double-strain, as the puree wouldn't be able to pass through the fine mesh strainer, so keep this in mind.

2 oz (60 ml) tequila reposado

1 oz (30 ml) mango puree (see introduction)

¾ oz (22 ml) fresh lime juice

½ oz (15 ml) Jalapeño Agave Syrup (page 162)

Garnish: Tajín rim and lime wheel

Take a slice of lime and rim the edge of a large coupe, and then rub it in Tajín or another spice blend. You can also only rim half of the glass, which allows a guest to avoid the spicy seasoning if they prefer. Place the rimmed coupe in the freezer to chill. Combine the tequila reposado, mango puree, fresh lime juice and Jalapeño Agave Syrup in a shaker and shake with ice. Loosely strain into your prepared coupe and serve up. Garnish with a lime wheel.

THE BARTENDER SUGGESTS
Pueblo Viejo Tequila Reposado
La Gritona Reposado
Libélula Tequila

POWER-UP TECHNIQUE

I'm going to let you in on a little secret—one of the best "power-ups" for a Margarita (page 39) is carrot juice. It likely doesn't sound all that obvious at first, but fresh, earthy carrot juice pairs incredibly well with agave spirits. For this Margarita twist, I split the base spirit to use equal parts of both tequila and mezcal. This is something you can easily do with a standard Margarita recipe as well or you can sub out the tequila completely for mezcal—up to you! Mezcal itself tends to add a nice smoky, savory element that is especially nice with carrot juice. Then fresh lime juice adds plenty of brightness to balance out the earthiness and, if you like it spicy (like I do), you'll love the Jalapeño Agave Syrup (page 162) used in this recipe.

Note that carrot juice is pretty difficult to make fresh unless you have a good quality juicer. Although fresh carrot juice really is amazing, you can go with store-bought here. Try to find carrot juice that is from the refrigerated section of a grocery store, as this will be closer to fresh juice vs. the shelf-stable variety.

1 oz (30 ml) mezcal espadin

1 oz (30 ml) tequila reposado

¾ oz (22 ml) carrot juice

¾ oz (22 ml) fresh lime juice

½ oz (15 ml) Jalapeño Agave Syrup (page 162)

Garnish: black sea salt and lime wedge

Take a slice of lime and rim half of the edge of a rocks glass, and then rub it in black sea salt (for a cool color contrast) or standard coarse sea salt. You can also only rim half of the glass, which allows the guest to avoid the salt rim if they prefer. Place the rimmed rocks glass in the freezer to chill. Combine the mezcal espadin, tequila reposado, carrot juice, fresh lime juice, and Jalapeño Agave Syrup in a shaker and shake with ice. Strain into your prepared rocks glass over fresh ice. Garnish with a lime wedge by placing it directly into the cocktail.

THE BARTENDER SUGGESTS

Banhez Mezcal Ensamble
Libélula Tequila

CLOVER CLUB

This classic recipe predates prohibition in the United States, so imbibers have been enjoying it for well over 100 years. Thanks to the drink's bright red color, its silky head of white foam and fresh raspberry garnish, it's certainly an eye-catching drink that often causes onlookers to say to the bartender, "I'll have whatever that is."

The Clover Club follows a very simple and recognizable sour format, with gin as the base spirit. The key ingredient here is freshly made Raspberry Syrup (page 162). Obviously, there are plenty of readily available store-bought raspberry syrup options, but as with many cocktail ingredients in this book, fresh ingredients tend to be the best option. It takes a little bit of effort, but making a syrup from fresh raspberries really does make this drink special. If you don't end up using it all on cocktails, just save it for breakfast and pour it over pancakes or waffles. You can thank me later.

1½ oz (45 ml) gin

½ oz (15 ml) fresh lemon juice

½ oz (15 ml) Raspberry Syrup (page 162)

1 egg white

Garnish: 3 raspberries skewered on a cocktail pick

Combine the gin, fresh lemon juice, Raspberry Syrup and egg white in a shaker and dry shake to break down the egg white. Open the shaker, add ice and shake again. Double-strain into a chilled coupe, serve up and garnish by placing three skewered raspberries on the edge of the glass.

THE BARTENDER SUGGESTS
Plymouth Gin
The Walter Collective Navy Gin

HONEY-BASIL GIN SOUR

Here's a twist on a Gin Sour (the classic sour build with gin as the base spirit) that can, of course, be enjoyed any time you can get fresh basil, but it's just perfect on the first warm day of spring. It uses a citrus blend of both lemon and lime juice, and leans on Honey Simple Syrup (page 161) as the sweetener for balance. If you don't have access to fresh basil, this cocktail would still be delicious without it, but gently muddling several large basil leaves in this drink really does give it an extra level of flavor that you must try yourself.

I also opted to do away with the egg white in this cocktail. Egg white is great for adding that velvety texture to cocktails, but I also like to explore other texture options that can be enjoyed by people who may have an egg white allergy or dietary restrictions. I used a form of bitters in this cocktail that also acts as a cocktail foamer (see The Bartender Suggests section below).

½ oz (15 ml) Honey Simple Syrup (page 161)

4–5 large basil leaves

1½ oz (45 ml) gin

½ oz (15 ml) fresh lime juice

½ oz (15 ml) fresh lemon juice

4–5 drops of cocktail foamer

Garnish: fresh basil leaf and bee pollen (you may need to avoid if you have allergies)

Add the Honey Simple Syrup and fresh basil leaves to a cocktail shaker and gently muddle. Add the gin, fresh lime and lemon juice and cocktail foamer and shake well with ice. Strain into a chilled coupe or Nick & Nora glass and serve up. Garnish by placing a fresh basil leaf on top of the cocktail with a light sprinkle of bee pollen.

THE BARTENDER SUGGESTS

Freeland Spirits Gin
Uncle Val's Botanical Gin
Ms. Better's Bitters Miraculous Foamer

RUNWAY MAGIC

For this twist on a Clover Club (page 44), I wanted to make a drink with a similar visual appeal by having that inviting red color, but with a slightly different flavor profile. So, for the Runway Magic cocktail, I infused a bottle of gin with hibiscus tea (see recipe on page 168). In addition to giving the gin a beautiful pinkish-red appearance, it also imparts some earthy but refreshing flavors that add to the complexity of the cocktail. I also use one of my favorite French liqueurs, yellow Chartreuse, which adds a mysterious bittersweet layer, making this an exciting and layered flavor experience.

Once again, I opted out of adding egg white and instead used coconut water to add some texture. It doesn't foam up quite like egg white or other foaming alternatives, but still adds a pleasant silkiness to the drink and helps bond the various ingredients together.

2 oz (60 ml) Hibiscus-Infused Gin (page 168)

¼ oz (8 ml) yellow Chartreuse

¾ oz (22 ml) fresh lemon juice

½ oz (15 ml) coconut water

½ oz (15 ml) Simple Syrup (page 160)

Garnish: lemon twist and maraschino cherry

Combine the Hibiscus-Infused Gin, yellow Chartreuse, fresh lemon juice, coconut water and Simple Syrup in a cocktail shaker and shake with ice. Strain out the ice and shake again without ice (this is known as a reverse dry shake). Double-strain into a coupe or Nick & Nora glass and serve up. Garnish with a lemon twist and a skewered maraschino cherry.

THE BARTENDER SUGGESTS
The Walter Collective Gin
Freeland Spirits Gin
Yellow Chartreuse

SPIRIT-FORWARD COCKTAILS

As previously mentioned, the general guideline is that if a cocktail contains any thick or foggy ingredients like citrus or cream, it should be shaken with ice. But what about stirring a cocktail?

The rule of thumb here is that if a cocktail is composed of primarily spirit, or all clear ingredients, it should be stirred with ice. This includes drinks like the Old Fashioned (page 52), the Negroni (page 76) and the Martini (page 64), all of which we will cover in this section. These kinds of cocktails are made with ingredients that intermingle easily, and do not require the more aggressive mixing involved with shaking. Stirring a cocktail provides much more control over chilling and dilution (as opposed to shaking) because it's much gentler and doesn't break down the ice as quickly. This is ideal for spirit-forward cocktails because the stirring process allows these drinks to maintain a velvety texture.

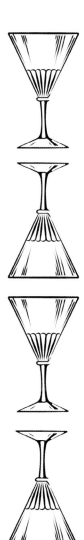

Add your ingredients to a cocktail mixing glass—if you don't have one, use a pint glass or even a French press. Ideally, you'll want a vessel with a wide base to ensure more surface contact with the ice. Fill the vessel with ice (use more than you think you'll need) and insert a barspoon down the side of the glass. Now gently pull the barspoon in a circular motion around the edge of the mixing vessel—try to use your wrist to stir and not your whole arm. Take care not to jostle the ice too much or add air bubbles, as this will change the texture of your final cocktail.

Feel the side of the mixing vessel occasionally with your other hand while stirring, and see if the cocktail is getting cold. Depending on the quality of your ice, 20 to 30 rotations is what you're aiming for before you're ready to strain the cocktail into your glass.

OLD FASHIONED

I like to refer to the Old Fashioned as the "classy grandpa" of mixed beverages. Back in the day it was simply referred to as a "cocktail," consisting of some sort of spirit, a bit of sugar, water and bitters. Pretty simple. As drinking culture developed, the word "cocktail" came to refer to any sort of mixed drink. So, in order to get this (now classic) concoction, people had to ask their bartender specifically for "an old fashioned cocktail."

Nowadays, if you walk into a bar and order an Old Fashioned, it's reasonable to expect a drink made from whiskey, sugar and bitters, served in a rocks glass and garnished with an orange peel and maybe even a maraschino cherry. However, depending on where you go, the drink you receive will vary wildly in terms of quality, as some regions make an Old Fashioned with muddled fruit and soda water. While you should make a drink however you like to enjoy it, the below ingredients and instructions are a widely accepted recipe for this beloved classic.

**2 oz (60 ml) whiskey
or brandy**

**1 tsp Demerara Syrup
(page 160)**

**4–5 dashes aromatic
bitters**

2–3 dashes orange bitters

*Garnish: orange peel and
maraschino cherry*

Combine the whiskey, Demerara Syrup and bitters in a mixing vessel and stir together with ice. Strain into a rocks glass over a large ice cube. Using a citrus peeler, cut a long strip of orange peel and gently squeeze it over the top of the drink (with the white pith facing toward you, not the drink). This releases a fine mist of citrus oil that will land on the surface of the drink. Then, drop the citrus peel directly into the drink, and add a skewered maraschino cherry.

THE BARTENDER SUGGESTS

Rittenhouse Bonded Kentucky Rye Whiskey
Peerless Kentucky Straight Bourbon
Angostura Aromatic Bitters
Luxardo Maraschino Cherries

SPICED APPLE OLD FASHIONED

It's incredibly easy to put your own twist on the Old Fashioned (page 52). By either swapping out the base spirit for another, or using a different kind of bitters or syrup, you can easily create a whole new drink. It's also a great recipe for making seasonally inspired cocktails (like this one for the autumn season). If you're making drinks for a party or creating a seasonal menu, a "Winter Old Fashioned" or a "Summer Old Fashioned" using seasonally appropriate ingredients is an easy win.

This recipe doesn't stray too far from the classic specs, but instead of a full 2 ounces (60 ml) of whiskey, I decided to split the base with calvados, a form of apple brandy from France. I also used a delicious homemade Spiced Simple Syrup (page 161). When combined with the whiskey and apple brandy, it makes it near impossible to not think about apple pie.

1 oz (30 ml) calvados

1 oz (30 ml) bourbon

¼ oz (8 ml) Spiced Simple Syrup (page 161)

3 dashes aromatic bitters

3 dashes sarsaparilla bitters

Garnish: apple fan and freshly grated cinnamon

Combine the calvados, bourbon, Spiced Simple Syrup and bitters in a mixing vessel and stir together with ice. Strain into a rocks glass over a large ice cube. Take a few thinly-sliced apple slices, fan them out and carefully place them next to the ice. They should stick together on their own, but you can also use a cocktail pick to keep them from falling apart. Finish the cocktail with a light dusting of freshly grated cinnamon.

THE BARTENDER SUGGESTS

Boulard XO Calvados
Laird's Apple Brandy Bottled in Bond
Coopers' Craft Barrel Reserve Bourbon
Honest John Sarsaparilla Bitters

OAXACAN INDIGO

This drink clearly doesn't look much like how you'd expect an Old Fashioned (page 52) riff to appear, but upon closer inspection, you'll notice the recipe follows the same basic format of spirit, a touch of sugar and bitters. I used mezcal as the base spirit for this twist, so there's a nice layer of smokiness to the drink. I also infused this Oaxacan agave spirit with butterfly pea blossom (see the recipe on page 169) which gives the drink a striking blue-purple hue—hence the name! The infusion is simply for aesthetic purposes, as butterfly pea flowers are nearly tasteless.

I really enjoy agave spirits, so I find them exceptional in Old Fashioned riffs, especially when there is a subtle spice element, like Jalapeño Agave Syrup (page 162). Some agave-based Old Fashioned riffs use a split base of both mezcal and tequila, so keep that in mind for further experimentation.

2 oz (60 ml) Butterfly Pea Blossom–Infused Mezcal (page 169)

1 tsp of Chareau aloe liqueur

1 tsp Jalapeño Agave Syrup (page 162)

4 dashes grapefruit bitters

Garnish: lemon peel and edible flowers (edible flowers are often purchased in a mixed variety; select whatever flower looks good to you!)

Combine the mezcal, aloe liqueur, Jalapeño Agave Syrup and bitters in a mixing vessel and stir together with ice. Strain into a rocks glass over a large ice cube. Using a citrus peeler, cut a long strip of lemon peel and gently squeeze it over the top of the drink (with the white pith facing toward you, not the drink). This releases a fine mist of citrus oil that will land on the surface of the drink. Discard the citrus peel. Take an edible flower and carefully balance it in the center of the large ice cube.

The Bartender Suggests

Banhez Mezcal Ensamble
Chareau Aloe Liqueur
The Bitter Housewife Grapefruit Bitters

HEAVY WEATHER

I made this original cocktail for a friend of mine, and he said that it was the best cocktail he ever had. That's some high praise, but I'll let you be the judge!

Heavy Weather splits the Old Fashioned (page 52) base three ways. I use an aged cachaça, which is a unique form of rum from Brazil. It's distilled from sugarcane juice and has a lot of funky fruit flavors and even some savory notes. The second component is Drambuie, which is a honey liqueur made from scotch whisky. The third spirit element is a bittersweet herbal liqueur made with Indian spices, like cardamom, black pepper and chai tea. The exact product isn't made anymore, but the cocktail is just as tasty with other commonly found bittersweet liqueurs, like Amaro Lucano.

It may be difficult to track down the exact ingredients I recommend for this cocktail, but ultimately that's okay. I hope this recipe can lead you to further experimentation; swapping out various ingredients and seeing what works for you. If you can't find aged cachaça, try a rhum agricole or even a Jamaican rum like Smith & Cross.

1 oz (30 ml) aged cachaça

½ oz (15 ml) Drambuie

½ oz (15 ml) chai-spiced amaro

1 tsp Demerara Syrup (page 160)

4 dashes cardamom bitters

Garnish: orange twist

Combine the aged cachaça, Drambuie, chai-spiced amaro, Demerara Syrup and cardamon bitters in a mixing vessel and stir together with ice. Strain into a rocks glass over a large ice cube. Using a citrus peeler, cut a long strip of orange peel and gently squeeze it over the top of the drink (with the white pith facing toward you, not the drink). This releases a fine mist of citrus oil that will land on the surface of the drink. Trim off the rough edges of the orange peel, give it a twist and place it in the drink.

THE BARTENDER SUGGESTS
Avuá Amburana Cachaça
Drambuie Liqueur
Townshend's Kashmiri Amaro
Amaro Lucano 1894
The Bitter Housewife Cardamom Bitters

SAZERAC

The creation of this classic New Orleans cocktail is commonly credited to a Creole apothecary from the early 19th century by the name of Antoine Amédée Peychaud. Before cocktails were even called cocktails, he was supposedly known for serving his own mixture of brandy and bitters in small cups called coquetiers. It has since become the cocktail that New Orleans is most known for, although it has taken on various additions and changes over the last hundred years. For example, the United States was largely cut off from Europe's supply of cognac and wine in the later part of the 19th century due to the phylloxera outbreak (a nasty pest that feeds on grape vines and roots), so rye whiskey was used to make Sazeracs instead as it was much more widely available at the time. I split the base in my Sazeracs, as many bartenders do nowadays, using both cognac and rye whiskey, so you get the best of both worlds.

You'll likely notice that a Sazerac is very similar to an Old Fashioned (page 52). The key components that differentiate a Sazerac are the use of Peychaud's bitters (named for the drink's creator) and an absinthe rinse. Peychaud's bitters are a form of bitters that have a bright red color and distinctive flavors of dark cherry, clove and anise that are supposedly modeled after Antoine Peychaud's original proprietary recipe. A Sazerac also wouldn't be a proper Sazerac without an absinthe rinse, which gives this potent cocktail a slight medicinal quality and black licorice aroma.

1 oz (30 ml) rye whiskey

**1 oz (30 ml) cognac
or brandy**

**1 tsp Demerara Syrup
(page 160)**

2 dashes aromatic bitters

**3 dashes Peychaud's
bitters**

Absinthe rinse

Garnish: lemon peel

Combine the ingredients in a mixing glass and stir with ice. Strain into a rocks glass that has been rinsed with absinthe and serve up. To rinse your glass, take a chilled rocks glass and pour ¼ ounce (8 ml) of absinthe into the glass and swirl it around, coating the inside of the glass before discarding the absinthe. Alternatively, you can fill a small spray bottle with absinthe and spray the glass several times with absinthe either before or after straining the cocktail. Using a citrus peeler, cut a long strip of lemon peel and gently squeeze it over the top of the drink (with the white pith facing toward you, not the drink). This releases a fine mist of citrus oil that will land on the surface of the drink. Either drop the peel into the drink as a garnish or simply discard it.

THE BARTENDER SUGGESTS

Rittenhouse Bonded Kentucky Rye Whiskey
Martell VS Cognac

SPICED CRANBERRY SAZERAC

This simple twist on a Sazerac (page 60) is perfect for the holiday season thanks to my Spiced Cranberry Syrup (page 161). Being a rather boozy cocktail, a Sazerac pairs nicely with rich and fruity flavors, which is why I often recommend ordering a Sazerac with your dessert. However, subbing out the standard Demerara Syrup (page 160) with Spiced Cranberry Syrup practically makes this cocktail a dessert itself. Not that it's overly sweet by any means, but the tart cranberry and various baking spices present in the syrup give this already delicious concoction added depth and complexity.

Classic Sazeracs are known to have a strong anise flavor component due to the absinthe rinse and Peychaud's bitters that are essential in making this well-known drink. I figured adding a star anise garnish would be an appealing visual that makes sense for this cocktail. Slightly singeing it before adding it to the drink gives off a pleasant aroma that is a mysterious precursor to what you are about to enjoy.

1½ oz (45 ml) rye whiskey

½ oz (15 ml) aged rum

¼ oz (8 ml) Spiced Cranberry Syrup (page 161)

2 dashes aromatic bitters

3 dashes Peychaud's bitters

Absinthe rinse

Garnish: smoked star anise

Combine the rye whiskey, rum, Spiced Cranberry Syrup and bitters in a mixing glass and stir with ice. Strain into a rocks glass that has been rinsed with absinthe and serve up. To rinse your glass, take a chilled rocks glass and pour ¼ ounce (8 ml) of absinthe into the glass and swirl it around, coating the inside before discarding the absinthe. Alternatively, you can fill a small spray bottle with absinthe and spray the glass several times with absinthe either before or after straining the cocktail. Take a whole star anise and briefly flame it with a match or lighter to release its aroma, then carefully place it directly into the drink as a garnish.

THE BARTENDER SUGGESTS
Knob Creek Rye Whiskey
Flor de Caña 7 Gran Reserva Rum

MARTINI

The Martini is quite possibly the most recognizable cocktail in existence. From the ubiquitous martini glass immortalized on signs and logos all over the world, to the well-known "shaken, not stirred" drink order from everyone's favorite British spy. Everyone knows what a Martini looks like, but there is a lot of fierce debate around how exactly you make a proper Martini. A truly classic Martini is made with gin, but it is also made with vodka on occasion for those who may not favor the taste of gin. Usually, the debate around Martini recipes revolves around how much dry vermouth is used in the cocktail. Dry vermouth can add floral and herbal elements to a Martini. Some prefer a 50/50 Martini made with half gin, half vermouth. Others prefer a much stronger beverage made by merely rinsing the glass in vermouth, then discarding and drinking chilled gin out of the same glass.

Although 007 famously orders his Martini "shaken, not stirred," this is also a point of contention among cocktail experts and enthusiasts. Since a Martini is composed of primarily spirit, it technically should be stirred, as shaking the drink would only add air bubbles and overdilute the beverage. Stirring a Martini is much less abrasive, giving it a silky-smooth mouthfeel. With all that said, enjoy your Martini however you like it! Here's my preferred specs, which is technically a 5:1 ratio of 5 parts gin to 1 part vermouth. An olive is a classic Martini garnish, which will give your Martini more of a savory or briny quality (or you can add olive brine directly into the drink making it a "dirty" Martini). Others might prefer garnishing their Martini with a lemon twist which imparts subtle citrus flavors to the drink.

2½ oz (75 ml) gin

½ oz (15 ml) dry
vermouth

*Garnish: skewered olive
or lemon twist*

Combine the gin and vermouth in a mixing glass and stir with ice. Strain into a chilled coupe, serve up and garnish with a skewered olive. Or, if you prefer, use a citrus peeler to cut a long strip of lemon peel and gently squeeze it over the top of the drink (with the white pith facing toward you, not the drink). This releases a fine mist of citrus oil that will land on the surface of the drink. Trim off the rough edges of the lemon peel, give it a twist and balance it on the rim of the glass.

THE BARTENDER SUGGESTS
Plymouth Gin
Sipsmith Gin
Ransom Dry Vermouth
Dolin Dry Vermouth

WAFER DREAMS

Wafer Dreams is a bit of a departure from your classic Martini (page 64) specs, and more of an attempt to redeem the reviled "dessert martinis" of the 1990s. During the Dark Ages of Mixology in the '90s and early aughts, everything served in a classic martini glass was dubbed a Martini— whether it bore any resemblance to an actual Martini or not. Think about casinos or big chain restaurant bars serving "choco-tinis" filled with creamy liqueurs and chocolate syrup. While most of these concoctions were pretty bad cocktails, there is something special about enjoying an adult dessert in liquid form.

Thankfully, you can just try Wafer Dreams, a cocktail that still looks like a proper grown-up ordered it at a classy bar, and yet it tastes like a boozy cookie. I infused vodka with brown butter (see recipe on page 170), which gives the spirit subtle flavors and aromas that tend to remind people of baking. Amontillado sherry provides a subtle nutty character, while the combo of Vanilla Bean Syrup (page 163) and over-proof rum brings in sweet baking spice elements.

2 oz (60 ml) Brown Butter–Washed Vodka (page 170)

½ oz (15 ml) amontillado sherry

½ tsp overproof demerara rum

¼ oz (8 ml) Vanilla Bean Syrup (page 163)

Garnish: stroopwafel

Combine the Brown Butter–Washed Vodka, amontillado sherry, demerara rum and Vanilla Bean Syrup in a mixing vessel and stir with ice. Strain into a chilled Nick & Nora glass. Serve up and on an appetizer plate with a stroopwafel on the edge of the plate as a snack.

THE BARTENDER SUGGESTS
Reyka Vodka
Lustau Amontillado Los Arcos Sherry
Hamilton 151 Overproof Demerara Rum

THE DUCHESS

RECIPE BY LYDIA MCLUEN

This simple twist on a Martini (page 64) just might become your new favorite. It's one that I make often at home for myself, and for friends who are open to exploring new-to-them spirits. My friend Lydia McLuen created this one while building out the bar program at an Icelandic-inspired bar concept. Instead of traditional gin, Lydia uses the Scandinavian spirit aquavit, which has rich notes of anise and caraway. It's an incredibly savory and potent spirit that does exceptionally well in Martini riffs. Lydia then pairs aquavit with bianco vermouth and fino sherry, which adds a touch of salinity.

For The Duchess, its simplicity is its strength. Just like any good Martini should be, it's elegant and uncomplicated. Even when Lydia was developing the drink, it didn't require much or any tweaking. Lydia told me, "I made it, I tried it . . . and I thought it was perfect," and I can't help but agree with her.

1½ oz (45 ml) aquavit

1 oz (30 ml) bianco vermouth

¼ oz (8 ml) fino sherry

Garnish: lemon twist

Combine the aquavit, bianco vermouth and the fino sherry in a mixing vessel and stir with ice. Strain into a chilled Nick & Nora glass and serve up. Use a citrus peeler to cut a long strip of lemon peel and gently squeeze it over the top of the drink (with the white pith facing toward you, not the drink). This releases a fine mist of citrus oil that will land on the surface of the drink. Trim off the rough edges of the lemon peel, give it a twist and balance it on the rim of the glass.

THE BARTENDER SUGGESTS

Brennivin Aquavit
Carpano Bianco Vermouth
Lustau Fino Sherry

MANHATTAN

Meet the whiskey drinker's Martini (page 64)—the Manhattan. Although the Manhattan and the Martini are two very different drinks in terms of overall flavor profile and color, you'll see that they are pretty much identical when you compare the recipes. Both drinks consist of a strong base spirit (gin or whiskey) balanced with a fortified wine (dry or sweet vermouth). By this point in the book, you should notice how most classic cocktails are much more similar to each other than they are different.

While there isn't nearly as much debate over the exact specs and process as there is for the Martini, the Manhattan certainly has room for customization. Whether you prefer it with bourbon or rye, or garnished with maraschino cherries or an orange twist, many bartenders and enthusiasts alike have their own personal twist on the Manhattan.

2½ oz (75 ml) rye whiskey

½ oz (15 ml) sweet vermouth

2 dashes aromatic bitters

Garnish: skewered maraschino cherries

Combine the rye whiskey, sweet vermouth and aromatic bitters in a mixing vessel and stir with ice. Strain into a chilled coupe glass, serve up and garnish by balancing several skewered maraschino cherries on the rim of the glass.

THE BARTENDER SUGGESTS
Old Overholt Bonded Rye Whiskey
Knob Creek Rye Whiskey
Molassario Rosso Vermouth
Luxardo Maraschino Cherries

NOCTURNAL BURN

One of my favorite, and easy, twists on virtually any whiskey-based cocktail is to swap out the whiskey for an aged tequila. I took it one step further with the Nocturnal Burn by taking a tequila añejo and infusing it with roasted cacao nibs (see recipe on page 169) to add a bittersweet chocolate element to the drink. This infused tequila was delicious when used in a traditional Manhattan (page 71) spec with sweet vermouth and bitters, but it was made even better once paired with a sweet and earthy chili liqueur.

The real showstopper is the flamed orange garnish, though. This method (which can easily be used with other cocktails as well) involves briefly igniting the citrus oils from an orange or lemon twist to add a pleasant burnt citrus aroma to the surface of the cocktail (see instructions below). As always, please exercise caution anytime you're handling a flame around alcohol. It's definitely worth trying out though, and it's a pretty easy way to impress your friends.

2 oz (60 ml) Cacao Nib–Infused Tequila Añejo (page 169)

½ oz (15 ml) chili liqueur

½ oz (15 ml) sweet vermouth

2 dashes orange bitters

1 dash aromatic bitters

Garnish: flamed orange peel

Combine the Cacao Nib–Infused Tequila Añejo, chili liqueur, sweet vermouth and bitters in a mixing vessel and stir with ice. Strain into a chilled coupe glass and serve up. Use a citrus peeler to cut a long strip of orange peel. Then, carefully light a match and hold it close to the rim of the cocktail. Hold the orange peel close behind the match and squeeze it over the flame. This will release a light mist of citrus oil that will briefly ignite and land on the surface of the drink, leaving a delicious aroma of burnt citrus. Give the citrus peel a little twist and balance it on the side of the cocktail as a garnish.

The Bartender Suggests

Roca Patrón Añejo
Ancho Reyes Chili Liqueur
Mulassano Rosso Vermouth

BLONDE BY NATURE

Can you still call it a twist on a Manhattan (page 71) if it's served in a rocks glass over a big cube? I think so—even if it breaks some of our loosely defined cocktail rules. Whether this drink is more of a Manhattan or just another Old Fashioned (page 52) variation, it's delicious no matter how you categorize it.

Cognac is an incredibly versatile and varied spirit, so feel free to experiment with different cognac varieties on this one. Although older cognacs (often labeled as VSOP or XO) are often thought of as fancier than younger cognacs, I find myself reaching for a cognac VS the most often. Younger cognacs might not have as much depth and richness to them, but they are still packed with incredibly bright and complex flavors that lend themselves well to all manner of cocktails. Because cognac is a spirit that is made from distilled wine, I purposefully used other ingredients that are made from grapes—including vermouth, a homemade red wine syrup (see recipe on page 164) and even absinthe.

2 oz (60 ml) cognac VS

¾ oz (22 ml) bianco vermouth

1 tsp Red Wine Syrup (page 164)

2 dashes absinthe

1 dash black walnut bitters

Garnish: orange peel and maraschino cherries

Combine the cognac VS, bianco vermouth, Red Wine Syrup, absinthe and black walnut bitters in a mixing vessel and stir with ice. Strain into a rocks glass over a large cube. Garnish by placing a nicely trimmed orange peel in the drink, along with several skewered maraschino cherries.

THE BARTENDER SUGGESTS
Martell VS Cognac
Mulassano Bianco Vermouth
Honest John Black Walnut Bitters
Luxardo Maraschino Cherries

NEGRONI

This Italian classic is either loved or hated and there seems to be no in-between. To be honest, I was in the hate camp when I first tried it, as this red and boozy cocktail is famously bitter and abrasive at first. But a good Negroni is like that one friend who's a bit rough-around-the-edges—as you get to know them, you not only accept them for who they are, but the things that first made them difficult to love start to feel endearing. That was a Negroni for me.

The Negroni has quite a loyal fanbase and there's even an annual Negroni Week where bars around the world serve Negronis and raise funds for various charitable organizations. Part of the Negroni's appeal is that it's a cocktail that is nearly impossible to mess up or "make wrong" unless you're purposefully trying to do so. It calls for equal parts gin, sweet vermouth and a bright red bitter digestif called Campari (the key ingredient). I will generally measure 1 ounce (30 ml) of each ingredient, but even if you just eyeball it and get somewhere close, your Negroni will still turn out alright. If you can't handle the bitterness at first, dial back the Campari a bit or even sub it out for its less abrasive cousin, Aperol.

1 oz (30 ml) gin

1 oz (30 ml) sweet vermouth

1 oz (30 ml) Campari

Garnish: orange peel or orange slice

Combine the gin, sweet vermouth and Campari in a mixing vessel and stir with ice. Strain into a rocks glass over fresh ice. Garnish by placing an orange peel or a fresh orange slice on the rim of the glass.

THE BARTENDER SUGGESTS

Plymouth Gin
The Walter Collective Navy Gin
Mulassano Rosso Vermouth

BOULEVARDIER

Here we have a situation where a twist on a classic cocktail has become a classic itself. A Boulevardier is nothing more than a Negroni (page 76) with the gin swapped out for a high-proof whiskey. Once again, it's a simple twist, but like the Negroni, the Boulevardier has inspired its own loyal fanbase. For whatever reason, many find the Boulevardier a little more approachable than the Negroni—possibly because a high-alcohol content bourbon can "push back" more strongly against the already pushy Campari. So, if you weren't a fan of the Negroni, try this one out and see what you think.

A Boulevardier is my personal go-to for "batching," meaning I easily premix Boulevardiers for special events or parties where I need to serve a lot of people. It doesn't contain any citrus or other perishable ingredients, so all the components are pretty much shelf-stable. With its simple, equal-parts build, it's easy to scale the recipe up or down based on the number of expected guests. For example, instead of mixing 1 ounce (30 ml) of each ingredient for a single cocktail, combine one full bottle of each ingredient and you'll have enough to serve 25 cocktails. Easiest party ever!

1 oz (30 ml) 100-proof
bourbon or rye whiskey

1 oz (30 ml) sweet
vermouth

1 oz (30 ml) Campari

Garnish: orange peel

Combine the rye whiskey, sweet vermouth and Campari in a mixing vessel and stir with ice. Strain into a rocks glass over fresh ice. Garnish by placing an orange peel in the drink.

THE BARTENDER SUGGESTS

Coopers' Craft Barrel Reserve Bourbon
Rittenhouse Bonded Kentucky Rye Whiskey
Mulassano Rosso Vermouth

TEQUILA NEGRONI BIANCO

A popular twist on a Negroni (page 76) is making a negroni bianco. Instead of using Campari and sweet vermouth, you swap in another type of bitter liqueur (like Salers Aperitif or Luxardo Bitter Bianco) that is clear in appearance, and use bianco vermouth (another form of sweet vermouth, but lighter in color). Since I'm an agave spirits fan personally, I took this twist a little further and swapped out the gin for tequila reposado, although I'm certainly not the first to bring forth this delicious combination. I used the classic equal parts recipe at first, but I felt like the tequila was getting ever-so-slightly overpowered by the bitter liqueur I was using. So, I adjusted the ratios by dialing back the bitter liqueur and vermouth and adding in a bit more tequila, and then it was nearly perfect.

You'll notice that many of my tequila or mezcal cocktail recipes incorporate some sort of spice or pepper element, and this recipe is no different. I got my hands on a nice bottle of shishito bitters, but instead of adding heat to the beverage, it more or less just added a subtle savory layer that truly completed this drink.

1½ oz (45 ml) tequila reposado

¾ oz (22 ml) bianco vermouth

¾ oz (22 ml) bittersweet gentian liqueur

3 dashes shishito bitters

Garnish: lemon twist

Combine the tequila reposado, bianco vermouth, bittersweet gentian liqueur and shishito bitters in a mixing vessel and stir with ice. Strain into a rocks glass over a large cube. Use a citrus peeler to cut a long strip of lemon peel and gently squeeze it over the top of the drink (with the white pith facing toward you, not the drink). This releases a fine mist of citrus oil that will land on the surface of the drink. Trim off the rough edges of the lemon peel, give it a twist and balance it on the rim of the glass.

THE BARTENDER SUGGESTS

La Gritona Reposado
Cocchi Americano Aperitif (Blanc Vermouth)
Salers Aperitif
Honest John's Celery-Shishito Bitters

TRY NOT TO BLUSH

I mentioned a negroni bianco previously as a popular twist—so how about a negroni *blush*?

This twist also centers around bianco vermouth and a clear bittersweet liqueur, like Salers Aperitif or Cascadia Liqueur. With the addition of a few dashes of Peychaud's bitters, this drink turns a lovely pale pink (or blush) hue. But where things really get interesting is with the combo of rhum agricole (rum distilled from fresh sugarcane juice, instead of molasses) and a unique brandy from Patagonia called TRÄ·KÁL. This concoction makes this twist on a Negroni (page 76) incredibly layered. It's no longer simply bittersweet, but also fruity, tart and somewhat vegetal all at the same time.

While the recipe departs from the tried and true "equal parts" spec of a classic Negroni, it's worth trying and experimenting with. If you can't find TRÄ·KÁL, a close substitute is pisco. Similarly, if you can't find rhum agricole, try making a similar riff using various types of rum—that is always a fun adventure.

¾ oz (22 ml) aged rhum agricole

½ oz (15 ml) Patagonian brandy

¾ oz (22 ml) bittersweet gentian liqueur

1 oz (30 ml) bianco vermouth

2 dashes Peychaud's bitters

Garnish: lemon twist

Combine the aged rhum agricole, Patagonian brandy, bittersweet gentian liqueur, bianco vermouth and Peychaud's bitters in a mixing vessel and stir with ice. Strain into a rocks glass over a large cube. Use a citrus peeler to cut a long strip of lemon peel and gently squeeze it over the top of the drink (with the white pith facing toward you, not the drink). This releases a fine mist of citrus oil that will land on the surface of the drink. Trim off the rough edges of the lemon peel, give it a twist and balance it on the rim of the glass or in the middle of the large cube.

THE BARTENDER SUGGESTS

Clement Select Barrel Rhum
TRÄ·KÁL Patagonian Spirit
New Deal Distillery Cascadia American Bitter Liqueur
Cocchi Americano Aperitif (Blanc Vermouth)

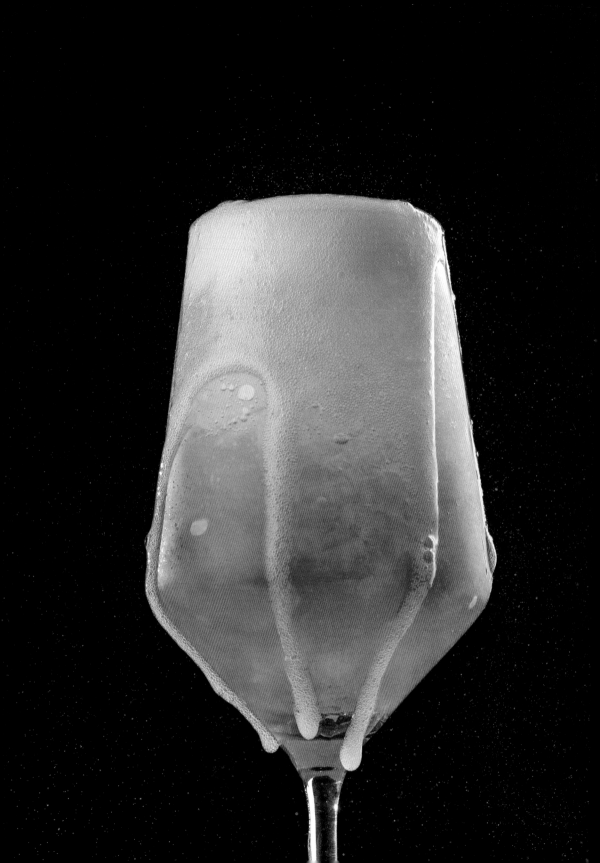

EFFERVESCENT COCKTAILS

Whether it's a simple two-ingredient tipple or a classy spritz with brunch, sometimes you just need a bubbly cocktail.

All the recipes in this chapter are loosely categorized by having this one thing in common: carbonation. The recipes' templates will vary quite a bit, as some are simple two- to three-ingredient drinks that you can mix in a glass, while others may involve shaking various ingredients first before adding the bubbles. Some use things like soda water or tonic, while others get their effervescence from champagne or another sort of sparkling wine.

As you'll soon find, bubbly or sparkling cocktails are some of the most forgiving when it comes to developing your own recipes. I, of course, include exact measurements for accuracy and consistency, but many of these drinks (like the Aperol Spritz [page 90]) are some of the very few cocktails where I'll tell you it's okay if you want to "just eyeball it." If you aren't an incredibly detail-oriented person, this is your section!

HIGHBALL

To some, the Highball is nothing more than an easy, nearly thoughtless cocktail involving pouring a bit of whiskey into a glass with some sort of sparkling liquid (usually soda water or ginger beer). That is by no means a bad approach—if that's your style, it works! But for others, especially bartenders in Japan who are known for popularizing the Whiskey Highball, this cocktail requires the highest quality ingredients, as well as time and attention to precise details.

The Japanese preparation of a Highball has been likened to a tea ceremony. There is a precise order and almost ceremonial process to be followed, and anything less simply won't do. In brief (although summarizing feels irreverent), the process involves taking a clear, hand-cut block ice and carving it down to size, then adding it to the glass and stirring until a light frost layer appears on the glass. Any water left over from the ice is drained out, the whiskey is carefully measured and added and the whiskey and ice are stirred precisely thirteen-and-a-half times clockwise. Then, more ice is added, filling the glass, and topped with soda water. This level of detail may seem unnecessary to your average imbiber, but there's something special to be learned in taking a simple drink and making it the absolute best it can be.

1 part whiskey

2 parts soda water or ginger beer

Garnish: lemon peel

Add standard ice cubes or a long, slender "ice spear" to a highball glass and stir until the glass is chilled. Using a barspoon to hold the ice in place, carefully drain out any excess water from the slightly melted ice. Carefully pour in the whiskey and briefly stir. If using standard-sized ice cubes, add more ice if needed, completely filling the highball glass, and top with soda water. Garnish with a nicely trimmed lemon peel.

THE BARTENDER SUGGESTS
Suntory Toki Whisky
Fever-Tree Soda Water

EMPRESS HIGHBALL

Twists on a Highball (page 86) are very common and widespread. Nearly anything served in a tall glass with bubbles can be referred to as some sort of Highball, and for that reason, it's an easy template to experiment with when you're just starting to create cocktail twists of your own.

The Empress Highball is still fairly simple (albeit with a few more ingredients and steps than an original Highball) but is immediately eye-catching, thanks to the striking color of Empress Gin, which is infused with natural botanicals like butterfly pea blossom. You can build this drink in the same glass you serve it in and give it a quick stir to combine, but shaking several of the ingredients together does help "wake up" the citrus and provides a much brighter and consistent drinking experience.

1½ oz (45 ml) Empress Gin

¾ oz (22 ml) fresh lemon juice

½ oz (15 ml) Simple Syrup (page 160)

3 dashes absinthe

3 oz (90 ml) grapefruit soda

Garnish: grapefruit peel and edible flowers

Combine the gin, fresh lemon juice, Simple Syrup and absinthe in a cocktail shaker and shake with ice. Take a highball glass, fill it with ice and add the grapefruit soda. Now, strain the cocktail into the glass on top of the grapefruit soda. Garnish with a grapefruit peel and edible flowers, if available.

THE BARTENDER SUGGESTS

Empress Gin
Pernod Absinthe
Fever-Tree Grapefruit Soda

APEROL SPRITZ

The Aperol Spritz is undoubtedly the most iconic recipe in the spritz category. It's bright orange–red color and bittersweet orange flavor are instantly recognizable and enjoyed all over the world.

In general, the spritz category is meant to be enjoyed as a precursor to a meal and is typically slightly bitter to help stimulate the appetite. A good spritz is also meant to be low in alcohol, with no more than 1 ounce (30 ml) of strong spirit involved, preferably less. Aperol itself is a bittersweet orange liqueur at a very low ABV of 11 percent, making this Italian aperitivo a great introduction to the category. It's incredibly easy to drink and is an ideal preface (or accompaniment) to either a morning brunch or a late-afternoon happy hour. It's also another rare cocktail that is nearly impossible to mess up. There is a precise way of making it, but even if you opt to simply combine equal parts of Aperol and prosecco over ice, you can't really go wrong.

3 oz (90 ml) prosecco

2 oz (60 ml) Aperol

1 oz (30 ml) soda water

Garnish: orange slice

Fill a wine glass with cracked ice. Pour the prosecco in the glass, followed by the Aperol. Top with a splash of soda water, and garnish by adding an orange slice directly into the glass.

SOLSTICE SPRITZ

Here's another example of a classic spritz. Although I refer to it as an "original recipe," this is a fairly standard combination of amaro (which refers to the larger category of Italian bittersweet herbal liqueurs), bubbles and other elements to make the ideal pre- or post-meal beverage. Just like many of the cocktails in this book, the spritz is a drink format where you can easily swap out ingredients, and simply changing the brand of one ingredient (i.e. using one specific amaro vs. another) will greatly alter the final result.

For this particular recipe, I favor Vecchio Amaro del Capo. It's made from a unique and secret blend of twenty-nine roots, flowers, herbs and other botanicals like bitter orange, anise, mint and licorice. Like many amari (plural for amaro), it can easily be sipped on its own, but I think it makes the perfect bittersweet base for an early afternoon spritz.

1½ oz (45 ml) tonic water

1½ oz (45 ml) prosecco

2 oz (60 ml) amaro

¾ oz (22 ml) bergamot liqueur

3 dashes black walnut bitters

Garnish: skewered olive and orange peel

Fill a rocks glass with ice. Add tonic water and prosecco first, and then add the amaro, bergamot liqueur and bitters second. Stir only briefly, and then garnish by taking a skewered olive and orange peel and placing them on the side of the rim.

THE BARTENDER SUGGESTS

Vecchio Amaro del Capo
Italicus Bergamot Liqueur
Honest John Black Walnut Bitters

WATERMELON SUGAR RUSH

I'm not sure the Italians would approve of me calling this original recipe a "spritz" as there isn't any bitter element, and for some, it might conjure up childhood memories of a watermelon Jolly Rancher. You're unlikely to ever find this on a drink menu in a café in Venice, but it's a truly delicious cocktail regardless.

Ideal for summertime when fresh watermelon is in season, this cocktail calls for using the fresh fruit to create a syrup as the sweetener (once you make this cocktail with it, make sure to save some for watermelon margaritas). This cocktail is also a bit higher proof than many spritzes since it uses Batavia Arrack as its main ingredient. This unique spirit is distilled from fermented sap from coconut flowers or sugar cane, depending on where it was produced (usually either India, Sri Lanka or Southeast Asia). It's worth hunting down a bottle or two to try, as it's difficult to suggest a good substitute. It has some similarities to rhum agricole with its really funky vegetal flavors, but some varieties of Batavia Arrack also have really light, floral elements that are reminiscent of various styles of gin.

1 oz (30 ml) Batavia Arrack

½ oz (15 ml) fresh lime juice

½ oz (15 ml) Fresh Watermelon Syrup (page 164)

¼ oz (8 ml) yellow Chartreuse

1½ oz (45 ml) sparkling wine

Garnish: mint

Combine the Batavia Arrack, fresh lime juice, Fresh Watermelon Syrup and yellow Charteuse in a cocktail shaker and shake with ice. Strain into a bulbed glass (basically a wine glass with a short stem, but a standard wine glass works too) with cracked ice. Top with sparkling wine and briefly stir. Garnish by placing a bouquet of fresh mint on the edge of the glass.

THE BARTENDER SUGGESTS
Batavia Arrack van Oosten
By the Dutch Batavia Arrack
Yellow Chartreuse

FRENCH 75

While technically a spritz, the French 75 is a popular classic that is really known as its own thing. If you find it on a cocktail menu, you'll likely see that it's made with gin as the base spirit, which is incredibly delicious (as long as you like gin). However, I prefer to make and order mine as it was originally intended—made with the French spirit of cognac.

Cognac is often thought of synonymously with fall and wintertime, and used in spirit-forward cocktails such as the Blonde by Nature (page 75). Although I do enjoy a boozy cognac beverage, this incredibly versatile spirit made from distilled wine is just as amazing in lighter, more refreshing cocktails. For this type of cocktail, I'd recommend using a younger cognac (often labeled "VS," which means they are aged for at least 2 years in French oak), which tend to have flavors and aromas of fresh stone fruit and subtle floral elements.

Fun drinking activity: Make two French 75s, one with gin and one with cognac, and see which one you prefer.

1 oz (30 ml) gin or cognac

½ oz (15 ml) fresh
lemon juice

½ oz (15 ml) Simple Syrup
(page 160)

3 oz (90 ml) champagne

Garnish: lemon twist

Combine the gin, fresh lemon juice and Simple Syrup in a cocktail shaker and shake with ice. Double-strain into a champagne flute and top with champagne. Serve up. Garnish by balancing a lemon twist on the edge of the glass.

THE BARTENDER SUGGESTS

The Botanist Islay Dry Gin
Martell VS Cognac

PERUVIAN 75

For this recipe, we're simply taking the French 75 (page 97) down to the South American country of Peru. Instead of gin or cognac, we're using pisco. Somewhat similar to cognac in that it is also produced from fermented grapes, pisco tastes absolutely amazing in a French 75 cocktail format. You can just do a straight-across swap with the spirit, or as we've done here, swap out a few other ingredients to give it a more unique twist.

Depending on where you're located, it may or may not be easy to locate some fresh passion fruit for this cocktail. Some specialty markets carry it, but personally, it's not something I come across in the store very often. Even though fresh is best, I tend to just order passion fruit syrup since I've found a brand I really like that makes a good one (see The Bartender Suggests below). You could also use standard Simple Syrup (page 160) or get wild and swap in another fruit-based syrup of your choosing (check out some recipes in the Syrups & Infusions chapter on page 159).

1½ oz (45 ml) pisco

½ oz (15 ml) fresh lime juice

½ oz (15 ml) passion fruit syrup

1 dash aromatic bitters

3 oz (90 ml) sparkling wine

Garnish: lime wedge

Combine the pisco, fresh lime juice, passion fruit syrup and bitters in a cocktail shaker and shake with ice. Double-strain into a stemmed wine glass and top with sparkling wine. Serve up. Garnish by placing a lime wedge on the edge of the glass.

THE BARTENDER SUGGESTS
Control C Pisco
Small Hand Foods Passion Fruit Syrup

BALTIC MIDNIGHT

This recipe is perhaps a closer reference to a champagne cocktail, which is made by dropping a bitters-soaked sugar cube into a glass of champagne. This produces a delightful fizzing effect, where the sugar cube continues to bubble and dissolve in the champagne (or another kind of sparkling wine if you prefer) as you sip. For this twist, I added 1 ounce (30 ml) of aquavit, which is essentially Nordic gin, so I felt like the recipe landed somewhere close to French 75 (page 97) territory.

Just like all the bubbly low-ABV recipes in this chapter, the Baltic Midnight is a great morning brunch cocktail. The name was inspired by my time visiting Northeastern Europe in the summer, where it's so far north that the sun never really sets that time of year. So even at midnight, it feels like it's daytime. This, combined with my strange craving for breakfast food in the late hours of the evening, made me decide that a "Baltic Midnight" was the best time of day.

1 oz (30 ml) aquavit

3 oz (90 ml) sparkling wine

1 sugar cube

4–5 dashes aromatic bitters

Garnish: lemon twist

Add the aquavit and sparkling wine to a champagne flute without ice. Hold a sugar cube on a cocktail napkin or barspoon and saturate it with a few heavy dashes of aromatic bitters. Drop the cube into the glass, and garnish by placing a lemon twist on the edge of the glass.

THE BARTENDER SUGGESTS

LINIE Aquavit
Angostura Aromatic Bitters

AMERICANO

No, it's not the popular coffee beverage. The Americano has been confusing bar guests for decades because this low-ABV cocktail bears absolutely no resemblance to the espresso drink of the same name.

The Americano is essentially a bubbly and sessionable (a term that refers to a drink being low in alcohol content, so it can be enjoyed in multiple "sessions") twist on a Negroni (page 76) served with equal parts Campari and sweet vermouth—but instead of gin, it's topped with sparkling water. This is my go-to drink for social events when I don't really feel like drinking, or when I'm starting out on a long bar-crawl and want to pace myself. You can drink these for quite a while before you feel any buzz whatsoever. Americanos are low in alcohol, pleasantly bitter and refreshingly effervescent. If you're okay with upping the alcohol content slightly, use the exact same specs but swap out the sparkling water for prosecco. Then, you'll have a Negroni Sbagliato.

1½ oz (45 ml) Campari

1½ oz (45 ml) sweet vermouth

1½ oz (45 ml) soda water

Garnish: orange slice

Combine the Campari and sweet vermouth in a highball glass full of ice. Top with soda water and garnish by adding an orange slice into the cocktail.

THE BARTENDER SUGGESTS

Aperitivo Cappelletti
Mulassano Rosso Vermouth

PALOMAR AMERICANO

RECIPE BY RICKY GOMEZ

Like I mentioned with the Americano recipe (page 102), some bar guests get confused when they see "Americano" on a cocktail menu, because they're thinking of the espresso beverage of the same name. Although the Americano cocktail and the caffeinated variety are two completely different things, world-renowned bartender Ricky Gomez made his own version that combines them.

Instead of soda water, Gomez adds cold brew coffee to the mix of Campari and sweet vermouth and serves it over pebble ice. Although it's no longer effervescent, this combination is addictive and surprisingly refreshing. That coffee and Campari pairing is something special, and it really shines in this low-ABV cocktail. You can find this version of an Americano on the menu at Palomar, Ricky Gomez's Portland-based bar that is an ode to his Cuban heritage.

1½ oz (45 ml) cold brew

1 oz (30 ml) Campari

1 oz (30 ml) sweet vermouth

Garnish: orange wheel (fresh or dehydrated)

Add the cold brew, Campari and sweet vermouth to a highball glass and add pebble or crushed ice. "Swizzle" by inserting a barspoon into the drink and rubbing quickly between your palms. Top with more ice (if needed) and garnish by placing an orange wheel in the glass.

THE BARTENDER SUGGESTS

Stumptown Cold Brew
Dolin Sweet Vermouth

GOLD FINGER

The red and bitter Campari tends to get all the attention when it comes to drinks like the Americano (page 102) and Negroni (page 76), but a fun alternative is swapping it out with another bittersweet liqueur called Suze. Suze is a French aperitif made with gentian root, which grows in certain mountain regions in Europe. It's certainly bitter and earthy, but somehow manages to still be pleasant and floral. I was once served by a bartender who compared Suze to a high-cocoa dark chocolate—not because it tastes like that, but simply because it's not for everyone. Some people will try it and gasp at how anyone could possibly stomach it, while others will savor it and wonder where it's been all their lives.

When combined with bianco vermouth and some sparkling water, this Suze-based Americano makes a delicious aperitif that will play tricks on your palate, making you think there are more ingredients involved than are actually present in the cocktail. I found a cardamom soda at a local grocery store that I use just for this drink, but you can just as easily use plain soda water and add a few dashes of cardamom bitters.

1½ oz (45 ml) Suze

1½ oz (45 ml) bianco vermouth

3 oz (90 ml) cardamom soda

Garnish: coarse sea salt and lime peel

Combine the Suze and bianco vermouth in a glass full of ice. Top with cardamom soda (or substitute soda water and a few dashes of cardamom bitters). Add a small pinch of coarse sea salt to the surface of the cocktail and garnish by placing a strip of lime peel on the edge of the glass.

THE BARTENDER SUGGESTS

Suze or Avéze Gentiane Liqueur
Mulassano Bianco Vermouth
The Bitter Housewife Cardamom Soda

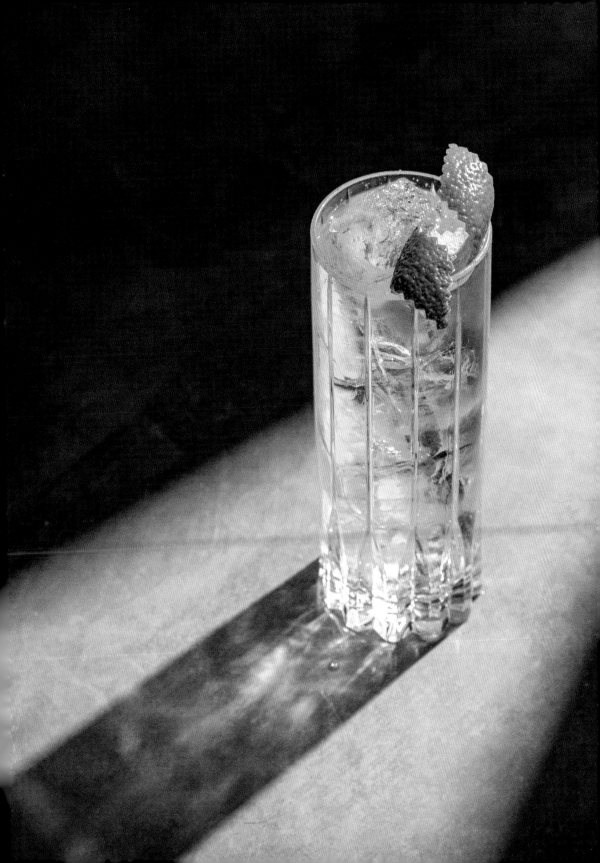

RAMOS GIN FIZZ

No one forgets their first Ramos Gin Fizz—it's truly a unique experience. It's sweet, thick and creamy, and there's not really anything else quite like it in the canon of classic cocktails. They're easy to enjoy, but difficult to make. This one will likely take some practice to get just right.

A few things to keep in mind: Different gins will change the overall experience. One recommendation is using Plymouth Gin, which will make your Ramos a little more on the citrus-forward side of things. But the classic recipe calls for Old Tom gin, which has been aged in oak and has some natural sweetness from the barrel. Another core element to this cocktail is achieving that perfect, foamy head. Make sure you're using fresh egg white for the best results, and after shaking and pouring, try placing the cocktail in the freezer to allow the foam to set. This will help it maintain its shape when you pour in the soda water, allowing it to rise above the rim of the glass.

2 oz (60 ml) gin

¾ oz (22 ml) heavy cream

½ oz (15 ml) fresh lemon juice

½ oz (15 ml) fresh lime juice

3 dashes orange flower water

1 fresh egg white

1–2 oz (30–60 ml) soda water

Combine the gin, heavy cream, fresh lemon and lime juice, orange flower water and egg white in a cocktail shaker and vigorously dry shake (without ice) for 20 to 30 seconds. Add ice and shake vigorously once more. Some bartenders will add only a single chunk of ice when shaking a Ramos Gin Fizz and shake it until the ice completely melts. This helps the cocktail get extra foamy. Then, double-strain into a collins glass. Let the cocktail sit for a few seconds to allow the foam to settle, or even place it in your freezer to help with this. Add soda water to your shaker tin and twirl it around to pick up any residual cream or foam on the sides of the shaker. Then, pour the soda water from your shaker tin into the center of your cocktail until a bit of the foamy head sticks up over the rim of the glass. Carefully insert a straw into the middle of the cocktail.

The Bartender Suggests

Ransom Old Tom Gin
Aviation Old Tom Gin
Plymouth Gin

PIE HOLE FIZZ

RECIPE BY JESSICA BRAASCH

A Ramos Gin Fizz (page 109) is already a fun (although labor-intensive) drink to make, but one of my bartender friends, Jessica Braasch, has succeeded in making this drink even more fun and delicious. Allow me to introduce her original twist on a Ramos: the Pie Hole Fizz.

This is one of few cocktails where I took a sip, stopped in my tracks and said out loud, "Oh wow, that's good." It's still made with Old Tom gin, just like the original Ramos Gin Fizz, but it incorporates other ingredients that will give you all the fall vibes. And instead of using plain old soda water, Braasch uses pumpkin beer as the bubbly element. Think pumpkin pie on Thanksgiving served with fresh whipped cream but in a liquid, boozy form, and that is essentially this cocktail. It's definitely a more decadent beverage that can be enjoyed in place of dessert, but I promise you one thing: It is 100 percent worthy of your indulgence.

1½ oz (45 ml) Old Tom Gin

½ oz (15 ml) amaretto

¾ oz (22 ml) allspice dram

½ oz (15 ml) fresh orange juice

½ oz (15 ml) heavy cream

½ oz (15 ml) Rich Simple Syrup (page 160)

1–2 oz (30–60 ml) pumpkin beer

Garnish: freshly grated nutmeg

Combine the gin, amaretto, allspice dram, fresh orange juice, heavy cream and Rich Simple Syrup in a cocktail shaker and vigorously dry shake (without ice). Add ice and shake vigorously once more, until well chilled and the outside of the shaker begins to frost over. Double-strain into a collins glass. Let the cocktail sit for a few seconds to allow the foam to settle, or even place it in the freezer for a minute to help the foam set. Add the pumpkin beer to your shaker tin and twirl it around to pick up any residual cream or foam. Then, pour the pumpkin beer from your shaker tin into the center of your cocktail until a bit of the foamy head sticks up over the rim of the glass. Top with freshly grated nutmeg, and then carefully insert a straw into the middle of the cocktail.

THE BARTENDER SUGGESTS

Ransom Old Tom Gin
Elysian Night Owl Pumpkin Beer
St. Elizabeth Allspice Dram

SIMPLE BUILDS

Making quality cocktails requires attention to detail, some basic bar tools and a base knowledge of various techniques. However, there are some beloved cocktail recipes that have stood the test of time while also being incredibly simple.

The following drink recipes require very few (if any) bar tools to make. For the most part, if you have a jigger or a shot glass to measure with and then something for stirring (like a barspoon or even a chopstick) you should be good to go. No cocktail shaker or mixing glass? No problem. All these cocktails can be built within the same glass you serve them in.

Just because these recipes are simple doesn't mean you should just rush through them or toss them together (but hey, if you have a crowd to serve, by all means bust some of these recipes out!). Similar to the way Japanese bartenders treat the Highball (page 86), even making a simple cocktail can be a thoughtful ritual that can give your guests a meaningful experience. For example, anyone can make a Gin & Tonic (page 118) simply by adding gin to tonic water, but by taking a bit more time and care to choose unique garnishes, or select a premium tonic, you can elevate a mediocre drink experience to a transcendent one.

MINT JULEP

Mint Juleps will likely make most people think of racehorses and fancy hats, as it's the signature drink of the Kentucky Derby, but this refreshing and spirited beverage is one you should be making even if you're nowhere near Kentucky.

I like to think of a Mint Julep as a "Summer Old Fashioned" (see Old Fashioned recipe on page 52). That might sound like a somewhat ridiculous comparison, but if you look at the recipe, that's essentially what you have. The cocktail is primarily made of bourbon and not much else, so you want to make sure you use a good one that you really enjoy. Since this drink is served over crushed ice (making it ideal to enjoy on a hot summer day at the racetrack), it's also best to use a bourbon that is at a bit higher proof. Since crushed ice melts quickly, a high-proof bourbon will ensure you still have a spirited and flavorful beverage as the ice melts.

8 large mint leaves

¼ oz (8 ml) Simple Syrup (page 160)

2 oz (60 ml) bourbon

Garnish: fresh mint sprig and aromatic bitters

In a julep cup (or rocks glass) gently muddle the mint leaves in the Simple Syrup. Add the bourbon, and then pack the cup with crushed ice. Stir until the cup is frosted over. Top with more crushed ice and form it into a dome. Garnish by placing a bouquet of mint in the drink and top with a few dashes of aromatic bitters on the surface.

THE BARTENDER SUGGESTS
Old Forester 100 Proof Kentucky Bourbon
Coopers' Craft Barrel Reserve Bourbon

SOUL CRAFT

You may have noticed that one of my favorite twists on classic whiskey cocktails is subbing the whiskey out for aged tequila. While this substitution may not always work for every cocktail, it really does well here.

I used a tequila cristalino añejo, which is an aged tequila that has been filtered in such a way to remove the dark color from the barrel aging, but without removing its depth and rich flavors of barrel spices and vanilla. I also added amontillado sherry and falernum to the mix to further emphasize some of the tequila's sweet, and even nutty, characteristics. Then for the finishing touch, I grated some tonka bean on top. Tonka beans might be unfamiliar to some readers but they are worth sourcing from a specialty spice shop or online suppliers. They are a unique South American legume that impart a vanilla and almond-like flavor when grated.

8 large mint leaves

¼ oz (8 ml) falernum

1½ oz (45 ml) tequila cristalino añejo

¼ oz (8 ml) amontillado sherry

Garnish: fresh mint sprig and tonka bean

In a julep cup or rocks glass, gently muddle the mint leaves in the falernum. Add the tequila and sherry, and then pack the cup with crushed ice. Stir until the cup is frosted over. Top with more crushed ice and form it into a dome. Garnish by placing a bouquet of mint in the drink and topping with freshly grated tonka bean.

THE BARTENDER SUGGESTS

Tequila Don Ramón Platinium Cristalino Añejo
Lustau Amontillado Los Arcos Sherry

GIN & TONIC

It's the ultimate lazy bartender's cocktail—tied only with the Jack & Coke, but somehow the Gin & Tonic feels a bit classier. You certainly can just add tonic and gin to a glass full of ice and toss in a lime wedge. If you're serving drinks at a sports stadium or on an airplane, that works just fine, but part of the appeal (and fun) of mixology is *crafting* a beverage—making something intentional and designed for someone to enjoy. So why not give a bit more effort than just the minimum that is required?

Personally, I enjoy making and serving Spanish Gin & Tonics, which is to serve a G&T similarly to how it is served in the Basque region of Spain. Instead of the typical lime or lemon wedge, you're more likely to see a Spanish G&T served with a colorful variety of garnishes that work in harmony with the gin, like orange peel, rosemary, juniper berries and pink peppercorns like I use here. Whatever gin you are using, follow that gin's existing flavor profile as your guide. For example, one of my favorite gins is from The Walter Collective, which still has a nice hit of juniper, but is also very citrus and spice forward, with notes of grapefruit, cassia and cardamom. I serve Gin & Tonics in a stemmed, bulbed glass, which are actually made for Spanish-style Gin & Tonics but you can also use a snifter or wine glass. I like to add a long strip of grapefruit peel, and various spices that complement or bring out the flavors already in that specific gin.

2 oz (60 ml) gin

4 oz (120 ml) tonic water

Garnish: orange peel and/or seasonal garnishes

Combine the gin and tonic water in a stemmed, bulbed glass and fill with ice. Garnish with an orange peel and your seasonal garnishes of choice.

THE BARTENDER SUGGESTS

The Botanist Islay Dry Gin
The Walter Collective Gin
Fever-Tree Tonic Water

ELDERFLOWER TONIC

The Gin & Tonic (page 118) is easy to twist and make your own. One of my favorite bars serves their house G&T with coconut-infused gin and a slice of pineapple for a tropical take. Whether you decide to add colorful and aromatic garnishes, or experiment with unique infusions, there is plenty of room for creativity.

One of the more widely known twists on a classic Gin & Tonic is adding some elderflower liqueur to the mix. It's not a huge change, but the presence of this incredibly floral sweetener does seem to pair with nearly any and all varieties of gin and gives this basic beverage an extra "something-something" that is sure to be a crowd pleaser. I prefer to dress mine up even further by adding a bit of absinthe and a few drops of grapefruit bitters, and I even garnish with some actual elderflowers whenever they are in season. A large slice of pink grapefruit also does well here but feel free to use whatever citrus you prefer.

1½ oz (45 ml) gin

¾ oz (22 ml) elderflower liqueur

1 tsp absinthe

2–3 drops of grapefruit bitters

3 oz (90 ml) tonic water

Garnish: grapefruit slice and/or fresh elderflowers

Combine the gin, elderflower liqueur, absinthe, grapefruit bitters and tonic water in a glass full of ice. If necessary, briefly stir to combine. Add a slice of fresh grapefruit directly into the glass as a garnish. If available, add fresh elderflowers to the rim of the glass.

THE BARTENDER SUGGESTS
Plymouth Gin
St. Germain Elderflower Liqueur

MOJITO

The Mojito is a cocktail where you can ask for one in nearly any bar and they'll be able to make it for you. Originally from Cuba, this refreshing rum cocktail is widely loved and enjoyed all over the world. But with the combination of the Mojito being a "knee jerk" drink order for many consumers and it being more labor-intensive (typically requiring muddling fresh mint), it is sometimes reviled by bartenders. Despite its popularity, the Mojito is not always the easiest cocktail to make. Some bartenders and enthusiasts alike will add too much mint, making the cocktail taste only of that one element. Even worse, some people will overly crush the mint when muddling, causing it to taste bitter. A good Mojito is light and refreshing with a soft kiss of mint that doesn't overpower the rum and lime. When done right, there's almost nothing better than a Mojito on a hot summer day.

3 large fresh mint leaves

½ oz (15 ml) Simple Syrup (page 160)

2 oz (60 ml) unaged rum

¾ oz (22 ml) fresh lime juice

2–3 oz (60–90 ml) soda water

Garnish: fresh mint

Add the mint leaves and Simple Syrup to a tall glass and gently muddle. Try not to rip the mint—just muddle it with slight twisting motions, enough to release the natural oils and that fresh minty flavor. Add the rum and fresh lime juice and top with crushed or pebble ice. Insert a barspoon into the drink and "swizzle" by rubbing the spoon quickly between both palms until the glass starts to frost over on the outside. Top with soda water and garnish by placing fresh mint in the glass.

THE BARTENDER SUGGESTS

Banks 5 Island Rum
Copalli White Rum
Probitas White Blended Rum

MEET ME IN BELIZE

Although this recipe is an obvious twist on a Mojito (page 122), I probably wouldn't describe the drink as such to a guest or if printing on a menu. My reasoning for this is because chocolate and banana are somewhat unexpected flavor additions to this cocktail, but let me reassure you that it's a twist worth exploring.

For this cocktail, I used one of my favorite rums from Copalli: a Belizean rum that is made with cacao and is grown at Copalli's own distillery in the rainforest, where they also grow their own organic sugarcane to produce their spirits. The rum itself is infused with freshly harvested cacao nibs and redistilled for an incredibly clean and delicious rum with rich chocolate flavors unlike anything I've ever tried. If you can't find Copalli Cacao Rum, you can try infusing some white rum with roasted cacao nibs by following the same process I outlined for the Cacao Nib–Infused Tequila (page 169). It will yield a slightly different result, but it will be a close substitute.

3 large mint leaves

½ oz (15 ml) crème de banane

2 oz (60 ml) cacao-infused rum

¾ oz (22 ml) fresh lime juice

1 oz (30 ml) spiced ginger ale

Garnish: fresh mint leaves and grated coffee

Add the fresh mint leaves and crème de banane to a tall glass and gently muddle. Try not to rip the mint—just muddle it with slight twisting motions, enough to release the natural oils and that fresh minty flavor. Add the rum and fresh lime juice and top with crushed or pebble ice. Insert a barspoon into the drink and "swizzle" by rubbing the spoon quickly between both palms until the glass starts to frost over on the outside. Top with ginger ale and garnish by placing fresh mint in the glass and use a microplane grater to top with freshly grated coffee.

THE BARTENDER SUGGESTS

Copalli Cacao Rum
Tempus Fugit Crème de Banane Liqueur
Fever-Tree Spiced Orange Ginger Ale

DARK & STORMY

As much as I preach the gospel of making quality cocktails and encourage others to really learn the techniques themselves, I am also not above enjoying the simple, shot-and-soda cocktails either—recipes like a Jack & Coke, Moscow Mule or the one I included here: a Dark & Stormy. These recipes just involve adding a shot or so of spirit to your soda of choice, along with some citrus. It's nothing complicated, but for many people, that's simply what they enjoy drinking and that's great. Let's banish the idea of the stuck-up, hipster bartender forever and not shame anyone for their preferred drink order.

Like the Highball (page 86) discussed earlier in this book, even the simplest cocktails can be made with intention and showmanship to make the experience more meaningful to the person you're serving. For an easy recipe like the Dark & Stormy, I like serving people a deconstructed version, where they receive a glass full of ginger beer, a lime wedge and a stylish glass container holding the rum. Then, they combine the ingredients as they see fit. They essentially are making the drink themselves, but it's a fun way to involve your guest in the drink-making process.

2 oz (60 ml) blackstrap rum

½ oz (15 ml) fresh lime juice

5 oz (150 ml) ginger beer

Garnish: lime wedge

Add the rum and fresh lime juice to a rocks glass or highball full of ice. Top with ginger beer and briefly stir. Garnish by placing a lime wedge on the edge of the glass.

THE BARTENDER SUGGESTS

Goslings Black Seal Rum
Reed's Extra Ginger Beer

HIGH FUNCTIONING

Did you know that pineapple and coffee make an incredible pairing? You heard it here first! Despite enjoying it as its own beverage, I tend to stay away from using coffee in my cocktails, but there are some flavor pairings that I just can't pass up and this is one of them.

This recipe is a great excuse to drink a rum cocktail when you're out to brunch in the morning. High Functioning combines pineapple juice and pineapple rum with coffee liqueur for a truly delicious and caffeinated flavor combo. It's the perfect balance of rich coffee and fruity sweetness with the perfect amount of bubbles to make it incredibly crushable.

1 oz (30 ml) pineapple rum

¾ oz (22 ml) coffee liqueur

½ oz (15 ml) pineapple juice

3 oz (90 ml) spiced ginger beer

Garnish: lemon and lime peels

Add the pineapple rum, coffee liqueur and pineapple juice to a rocks glass full of cracked ice and briefly stir. Top with ginger beer and garnish by placing both a lemon peel and lime peel on the edge of the glass.

THE BARTENDER SUGGESTS
Plantation Stiggins' Fancy Pineapple Rum
Mr. Black Coffee Liqueur
Fever-Tree Spiced Ginger Beer

WARM & SPIRITED COCKTAILS

Take some time to refill your ice molds and put away your cocktail shaker, because you won't be needing any of them for these recipes. The following cocktails are best served hot.

You may not have thought about it explicitly, but ice and water are key ingredients in the vast majority of cocktails. In shaken, stirred and built-in-glass cocktails, ice is used to chill the ingredients, as well as add the proper amount of dilution, which in turn, affects the texture or mouthfeel of the cocktail. Obviously, we are not working with ice when making hot cocktails, but it's still important to keep things like temperature and texture in mind. Hot cocktails rely on hot liquids like water, tea or coffee for temperature and dilution. Adding certain ingredients, like syrups or even some spirits, that tend to be stored cold can lower the temperature of your hot cocktails quickly so keep this in mind and try to allow them enough time to reach room temp before mixing with them. Then in terms of dilution, I try and stay around 3 to 4 ounces (90 to 120 ml) of hot water or other hot liquid to 2 ounces (60 ml) of spirit in each cocktail for optimal flavor and dilution. You can of course experiment with this, and go with whatever ratio you prefer.

Except for the hot cocktails made with "finicky" ingredients (like fresh espresso), most recipes are uncomplicated and can be easily made without a fuss. Whether you're camping in the woods or just need something extra to warm you on a cold winter's night, try some of these cocktails out.

HOT TODDY

Like many classic cocktails, the exact origin of the Hot Toddy is disputed. There are some records that suggest it originated in India, while others claim it was created by an Irish doctor to be given to patients. For a lot of early American history, the Hot Toddy was the cure for the common cold. Regardless of whoever was the first person to sip spirits in hot water, the Hot Toddy is undeniably the quintessential "hot cocktail."

There are abundant twists and variations on the Hot Toddy, but it's commonly made with whiskey or brandy, lemon juice, hot water and usually a bit of honey. Nowadays your doctor is unlikely to recommend a Hot Toddy, but even still, it's an enjoyable and comforting beverage to sip on when you're under the weather, or just need something to warm your bones.

Here's a hot tip (pun intended): Instead of just using plain old hot water, try various kinds of tea. My personal go-to is using Chai tea for Hot Toddies to add a nice, earthy spice element.

2 oz (60 ml) whiskey

½ oz (15 ml) fresh lemon juice

½ oz (15 ml) Honey Simple Syrup (page 161)

3 oz (90 ml) hot water

Garnish: lemon wheel

Preheat a tempered glass or mug with hot water. After about 30 seconds, remove the hot water and add the whiskey, fresh lemon juice and Honey Simple Syrup to the warm glass. Top with hot water. Garnish by placing a lemon wheel on the side of the glass.

THE BARTENDER SUGGESTS
Buffalo Trace Bourbon
Stranahan's Blue Peak Single Malt Whiskey

SCOTCH & WINE TODDY

This cocktail aims to combine two beloved warm beverages: the Hot Toddy (page 132) and mulled wine. It's very much a Hot Toddy variation, but thanks to my homemade Red Wine Syrup (page 164) and the addition of allspice dram, this Scotch & Wine Toddy can satisfy both cravings.

Although American whiskey is most often favored when making Hot Toddies, you'll find recipes that use all kinds of different base spirits. Personally, I really enjoy using scotch in my toddies, which (depending on the scotch used) can add a whole new depth and flavor to this simple drink. I wouldn't recommend using a high-end single malt scotch (save those for sipping) but there are some quality blended scotch options, or inexpensive single malts, that can add really diverse spice and floral flavors and aromas. Another base spirit suggestion for this Hot Toddy variation is to use apple brandy or cognac, as these other fruit-based spirits tend to pair nicely with the Red Wine Syrup.

1½ oz (45 ml) scotch whisky

1 oz (30 ml) fresh lemon juice

¾ oz (22 ml) Red Wine Syrup (page 164)

1 tsp allspice dram

3 oz (90 ml) hot water

Garnish: orange peel and whole cloves

Preheat a tempered glass or mug with hot water. After about 30 seconds, remove the hot water and add the scotch whisky, fresh lemon juice, Red Wine Syrup, allspice dram and hot water to the warm glass. Garnish by studding a long strip of orange peel with whole cloves. Place it directly into your drink.

THE BARTENDER SUGGESTS

Glen Moray Speyside 12-Year Whisky
Monkey Shoulder Blended Scotch
St. Elizabeth Allspice Dram

IRISH COFFEE

The Hot Toddy (page 132) might be the champion of hot cocktails, but the Irish Coffee must be a close second. Created by an Irish chef in the 1940s to be served to transatlantic travelers, the Irish Coffee started simply as whiskey-spiked coffee to ward off cold nights and has become a classic cocktail enjoyed all over the world.

A key element of this cocktail is the thin layer of hand-whipped cream on the surface. To make this, add the heavy whipping cream to a large bowl and whip it with a hand mixer. Be careful not to overwhip the cream as it needs to still be pourable. Stop every 10 seconds or so and remove the hand mixer. If there is a slight "peak" in the cream where you removed the mixer, the cream is likely ready.

1½ oz (45 ml) Irish whiskey

¾ oz (22 ml) Rich Simple Syrup (page 160)

4 oz (120 ml) black coffee

1–2 oz (30–60 ml) heavy whipping cream, lightly whipped

Garnish: freshly grated nutmeg

Heat a tempered glass with hot water. Remove the hot water and add both the whiskey and Rich Simple Syrup, and then fill the glass with black coffee. Leave about a ½ inch (1.3 cm) of space at the top for the cream. Top with a layer of lightly whipped heavy cream, making sure to pour it in slowly and carefully so it floats on top of the drink, and freshly grated nutmeg.

THE BARTENDER SUGGESTS
Slane Irish Whiskey
Teeling Irish Whiskey

CAFÉ FRANÇAIS

As far as I'm aware, this is not an authentic French cocktail—it simply became my personal twist on an Irish Coffee (page 136) after I started combining the French spirit of cognac with fresh espresso. Cognac has become a more recent love of mine, and I tend to prefer it now over whiskey in a lot of different cocktails. It's an incredibly versatile spirit that lends itself to all kind of different applications from spirit-forward nightcaps to bright and tropical cocktails, but there's no denying it's well-established strength as an after-dinner delight or an accompaniment to dessert.

You can certainly use black coffee here to put this recipe more firmly into Irish Coffee territory, but there's something about fresh espresso that is extra mind-blowing when combined with cognac. It goes without saying that you'll need an espresso machine for this one, or alternatively, you can order some espresso shots to-go at your local coffee shop. A milk frother will also come in handy in making the foam. Due to both the alcohol and caffeine content in this drink, it is certainly potent!

1½ oz (45 ml) cognac

1½ oz (45 ml) espresso

2–3 oz (60–90 ml) hot water

½ oz (15 ml) Spiced Simple Syrup (page 161)

3–4 oz (90–120 ml) whole milk

Combine the cognac, fresh espresso, hot water and Spiced Simple Syrup in a tempered glass (if you want it more concentrated, use less hot water). Carefully stir to combine. Using a steamer or electronic milk frother, heat and froth some milk. You can also do this by heating the milk in a microwave and whisking with a small handheld milk whisk. Then, scoop the foam onto the top of the cocktail.

THE BARTENDER SUGGESTS
Rémy Martin 1738 Accord Royal Cognac

TROPICAL COCKTAILS

Everyone loves and fantasizes about an island getaway–warm sun, a crystal blue sea and a break from the hustle and grind. In the days of the Great Depression in the United States, when international travel or any sort of indulgent vacation was nowhere near the realm of possibility for most Americans, the Tiki cocktail movement offered a sense of adventure and an escape from a bleak reality. Tiki bars served elaborate, over-the-top cocktails made with rum and unique ingredients in an atmosphere that sought to emulate exotic locales. Although both the bars and the cocktail recipes that emerged from the Tiki movement soon became kitsch in subsequent decades following WWII, Tiki still had a small but fiercely loyal base of enthusiasts throughout the years.

Interest in Tiki bars and cocktails has had a resurgence in popularity, but it's also had a fair share of criticism. There are some very real issues with cultural appropriation, as the whole Tiki movement was based on a caricature of Polynesian culture–created, perpetuated and enjoyed by largely white audiences. Several prominent bartenders of Pacific Island heritage are leading important conversations around this topic within the hospitality industry. There are a lot of hurtful elements of the Tiki craze that should be left to the past, while still appreciating the cocktail recipes that emerged from the movement.

Tropical cocktails have always been fun, usually made with rum (but not always), all kinds of bright and colorful ingredients and served with elaborate garnishes. Sadly, some recipes have devolved or been misconstrued over time, but you'll find several classic favorites here that are worth making as close to the original as possible.

MAI TAI

The Mai Tai is quite possibly the most iconic cocktail of the Tiki movement, but it is sadly also the most misinterpreted. This once simple drink, which is essentially a rum-based Margarita (page 39), has quickly devolved into a sugary mess made with bottled orange juice and served on board cruise ships and in tacky resort bars. It's one of those drinks where every time you order one, you'll likely receive something very different at each place you visit.

Back in the 1940s (when the Mai Tai was supposedly created by a man who went by the name Trader Vic), it wasn't a grossly sweet and syrupy concoction you only consumed on vacation. The Mai Tai was a balanced mix of fresh lime, orange curaçao, cane sugar and Orgeat (page 166), a nutty-almond based sweetener that was meant to perfectly complement the fruity and funky flavors of a 17-year-old J. Wray & Nephew rum. If you only know a Mai Tai from your last cruise ship experience, then you owe it to yourself to make a quality one.

2 oz (60 ml) aged rum

½ oz (15 ml) dry curaçao

¾ oz (22 ml) fresh lime juice

¼ oz (8 ml) Orgeat (page 166)

¼ oz (8 ml) Rich Simple Syrup (page 160)

Garnish: fresh mint and a lime hull

Combine the aged rum, dry curaçao, fresh lime juice, Orgeat and Rich Simple Syrup in a cocktail shaker with crushed ice, and briefly shake. Dump into a rocks glass and top with more ice, if needed. Garnish by placing a fresh bouquet of mint on top of the drink, as well as a spent lime hull (half a lime that has already been juiced). If you are feeling adventurous and really want to impress your guests, add a ¼ ounce (8 ml) of high-proof rum into the hollow lime hull and very carefully ignite with a match while still floating on top of the drink. Then, sprinkle a pinch of cinnamon over the flame for some added flare before blowing out the flame. As always, please be very, very careful if you decide to attempt this.

THE BARTENDER SUGGESTS

Smith & Cross Jamaican Pot Still Rum
Wray & Nephew White Overproof Jamaican Rum
Clairin Vaval Haitian Rum
Pierre Ferrand Dry Curaçao

PINEAPPLE TRAIN WRECK

RECIPE BY RYAN MAGARIAN

As I mentioned when talking about the Mai Tai (page 142), many bars serve their own version of the venerable classic. But unlike classics like the Old Fashioned (page 52) or Martini (page 64), where the exact specs are debated but the essential components are largely agreed upon, the Mai Tai seems to be much more open to interpretation—I've previously been served nothing more than rum-spiked pineapple juice after ordering a Mai Tai. Every bar or bartender's version of the Mai Tai tends to be so drastically different to a point where it's hard to really say what exactly makes a Mai Tai a true Mai Tai.

Thankfully this twist on a Mai Tai, created by my friend and renowned bartender Ryan Magarian, sticks close to the classic Mai Tai realm but is subtly modified with pineapple juice and a fresh ginger kick. There are some cocktails that I simply describe as "crushable," meaning they are so perfectly balanced and delicious that you could drink them all at once without even thinking about it. For me, the Pineapple Train Wreck has become the archetype of that definition, perhaps even more so than a classic Mai Tai—but don't take my word for it.

1½ oz (45 ml) aged rum

½ oz (15 ml) overproof rum

1½ oz (45 ml) pineapple juice

½ oz (15 ml) fresh lime syrup

¾ oz (22 ml) Spicy Ginger Syrup (page 163)

1 dash Peychaud's bitters

1 dash aromatic bitters

Garnish: pineapple frond and maraschino cherry

Combine the aged rum, overproof rum, pineapple juice, lime syrup, Spicy Ginger Syrup and bitters in a cocktail shaker and shake with ice. Strain over fresh ice in a rocks glass. Garnish by placing the pineapple frond in the drink, as well as a skewered maraschino cherry.

THE BARTENDER SUGGESTS

Plantation Original Dark Rum
Plantation O.F.T.D. Overproof Rum
Luxardo Maraschino Cherries

JUNGLE BIRD

The Jungle Bird is relatively "young" as far as classic cocktails are concerned, and undoubtedly many a bartender might scoff at me for referring to it as such. It came into existence as early as 1978 and was supposedly served as the welcome cocktail at the Kuala Lumpur Hilton. Compared to most citrusy tropical cocktails, the Jungle Bird was a bit of an odd duck as it contains the bitter Italian liqueur, Campari. However, this bright red cocktail continued to catch the attention of various bartenders throughout the years.

Largely thanks to NYC's Giuseppe González, who adjusted the initial specs of the Jungle Bird by dialing back the amount of pineapple juice and pairing it with rich blackstrap rum, the Jungle Bird has been plucked out of near-obscurity and is now widely known and enjoyed in bars and homes everywhere. The Jungle Bird is one of my personal favorite welcome cocktails to serve guests, as it seems to easily appeal to a wide range of palates. It's also my go-to cocktail to serve to anyone who says that they "don't like Campari" because it's basically guaranteed to change their mind.

1½ oz (45 ml) blackstrap rum

¾ oz (22 ml) Campari

1½ oz (45 ml) pineapple juice

½ oz (15 ml) fresh lime juice

½ oz (15 ml) Demerara Syrup (page 160)

Garnish: pineapple fronds, pineapple wedge and maraschino cherries

Combine the blackstrap rum, Campari, pineapple juice, fresh lime juice and Demerara Syrup in a cocktail shaker and shake with ice. Strain into a rocks glass and fill with cracked ice. Garnish by placing several pineapple fronds in the drink, and by placing a pineapple wedge on the edge of the glass with several skewered maraschino cherries.

THE BARTENDER SUGGESTS
Cruzan Blackstrap Rum
El Dorado 12-Year Demerara Rum

HIGH REGARD

This recipe has a lot of similar ingredients and flavors to the Jungle Bird (page 146), but the most significant change is how it takes the base spirit (rum) and the bitter component (amaro) and swaps the proportions. For those who denounce tropical cocktails for typically being too sweet and cloying, this is the recipe to make for them. Despite it being a lot heavier on the bitter side of things, a High Regard is still perfectly refreshing and bright thanks to both the fresh lime juice and Pineapple Demerara Syrup (see recipe on page 165).

When you mix one up, you'll likely notice the color of the drink itself is fairly dark, largely thanks to the heavy pour of amaro. This dark brown appearance may seem counterintuitive or even unappetizing to some for a tropical-style beverage, so that's where having some fun Tiki mugs are helpful. Tropical mugs and novelty glassware were and continue to be a fixture of the Tiki movement. Many vintage mugs and glasses are hard to find and are expensive—however, you can still get lucky at thrift stores occasionally. Thanks to a renewed interest in the category, there are various retailers that are producing new Tiki mugs that are more widely available. Some favorites from my personal collection include a yellow pufferfish mug and a 32-ounce (945-ml) ceramic conch shell.

1½ oz (45 ml) amaro

½ oz (15 ml) Jamaican rum

¼ oz (8 ml) allspice dram

¾ oz (22 ml) fresh lime juice

¾ oz (22 ml) Pineapple Demerara Syrup (page 165)

Garnish: pineapple fronds, fresh mint and powdered sugar

Combine the amaro, Jamaican rum, allspice dram, fresh lime juice and Pineapple Demerara Syrup in a cocktail shaker and shake with ice. Strain into a glass (or fun tropical drinking vessel of your choice) and fill with crushed ice. Garnish by placing a few pineapple fronds and fresh mint on the side of the glass. Top with a light dusting of powdered sugar.

THE BARTENDER SUGGESTS
Braulio Amaro
Smith & Cross Jamaican Pot Still Rum
St. Elizabeth Allspice Dram

PIÑA COLADA

Multiple bartenders from both Puerto Rico and Cuba have laid claim to being the first to combine rum, cream of coconut and pineapple together, but as is the case with the majority of cocktail history, the details and facts tend to be a bit hazy—which is fitting since alcohol is involved. We may never truly know who was the first, but it's pretty safe to say that this simple combination has been enjoyed long before the days of what we now call "mixology."

The Piña Colada is often enjoyed frozen as more of a slushie. If I were to magically find myself lounging on a beach in Mexico, that's exactly how I would order my Piña Colada as well. If you don't want to pull out the blender though, a Piña Colada is just as enjoyable made in a cocktail shaker with crushed ice. It's also another one of those somewhat rare cocktails where the exact measurements don't matter all that much. If you have a strong rum, a healthy pour of pineapple juice and a dollop of coconut cream, you're good to go!

2 oz (60 ml) your choice of rum

1½ oz (45 ml) cream of coconut

1½ oz (45 ml) pineapple juice

½ oz (15 ml) fresh lime juice

Garnish: pineapple wedge and pineapple fronds

Combine the rum, cream of coconut, pineapple juice and fresh lime juice in a cocktail shaker with pebble or crushed ice and briefly shake. Dump into a tall glass and top with more ice as needed. Garnish with a pineapple wedge and several pineapple fronds.

THE BARTENDER SUGGESTS
Copalli White Rum
Appleton Estate Rum
Wray & Nephew White Overproof Jamaican Rum

VIKING COLADA

RECIPE BY DANGUOLE LEKAVICIUTE

My friend and fellow creative, Danguole Lekaviciute, developed this recipe for a special event; and I was so intrigued when I first saw the drink, I just had to try it myself. I've talked about the Scandinavian spirit of aquavit in several recipes in this book like The Duchess (page 68) and Baltic Midnight (page 101). It tends to be anise and caraway-forward, and lends itself to more savory applications, which makes its use in this creamy cocktail unexpected. Also, seeing "root beer syrup" on a list of ingredients gives you yet another reason to do a double-take.

As odd as it might initially sound, this unique combination of flavors is a worthwhile adventure. It's an exciting mesh of a savory spirit with sweet and creamy ingredients, balanced with tart lime juice, and served over crushed ice. I'd suggest trying it out with Krogstad Aquavit, which is widely available in many regions. This drink may look like a Piña Colada (page 150) but it's something else entirely.

2 oz (60 ml) aquavit

¾ oz (22 ml) fresh lime juice

½ oz (15 ml) cream of coconut

½ oz (15 ml) root beer syrup

Garnish: fresh mint and maraschino cherries

Combine the aquavit, fresh lime juice, cream of coconut and root beer syrup, and shake with ice. Strain into a tall glass and fill with crushed ice. Garnish by placing a fresh bouquet of mint on the top, along with several skewered maraschino cherries.

THE BARTENDER SUGGESTS
Krogstad Aquavit
Coco Lopez Coconut Crème
Portland Syrup Co. Root Beer Syrup

ZOMBIE

If you happen to find yourself in what could only be described as a Tiki bar, you will likely see a Zombie on the menu with a safety warning highlighted in red text: "Limit two per customer." This is a fun gimmick that goes back to the Zombie's original creation in 1933 by one of the Tiki movement's earliest proponents and restauranteurs: Donn Beach. Although there isn't necessarily a legitimate safety concern around the Zombie, it is a hefty drink that contains 4 total ounces (120 ml) of rum consisting of three different varieties. So, limiting yourself to two (or even just one) is probably sound advice.

The cocktail recipe has been subtly tweaked over the years, so the exact specs will vary depending on who you ask. At first glance, it may look like a mess of random ingredients (just ½ ounce [15 ml] of grapefruit juice? Grenadine [page 166]?!) but if you want the true Zombie experience, don't skip any details. If you're unfamiliar with tropical cocktails, this one will show you just how much of an adventure they can truly be.

1½ oz (45 ml) Jamaican rum

1½ oz (45 ml) Puerto Rican rum

1 oz (30 ml) 151-proof demerara rum

¾ oz (22 ml) fresh lime juice

½ oz (15 ml) fresh grapefruit juice

½ oz (15 ml) falernum

¼ oz (8 ml) Grenadine (page 166)

2 dashes aromatic bitters

2 dashes Herbsaint or absinthe

Garnish: fresh mint, lime wheel and maraschino cherries

Combine the Jamaican, Puerto Rican and 151-proof rums with fresh lime juice, fresh grapefruit juice, falernum, Grenadine, aromatic bitters and Herbsaint in a cocktail shaker with pebble or crushed ice, and briefly shake. Dump into a tall glass and top with more ice as needed. Garnish by placing a fresh bouquet of mint on top of the drink. Add a lime wheel on the rim of the glass, as well as skewered maraschino cherries.

THE BARTENDER SUGGESTS

Wray & Nephew White Overproof Jamaican Rum
Flor de Caña 7 Gran Reserva Rum
Hamilton 151 Overproof Demerara Rum
BG Reynolds Falernum Syrup

CLASSY ZOMBIE

While the Zombie (page 154) is nearly 100 years old and is an incredibly fun cocktail experience, it is hardly a template for experimentation. It has a lot of ingredients and even swapping out just one or two of those building blocks will change the drink. A client of mine challenged me to come up with my own twist on a Zombie though, and the result ended up having more in common with an Old Fashioned (page 52) than an actual Zombie cocktail.

In true tropical-Tiki fashion, the Zombie is big, boozy and over-the-top. However, I thought it would be fun to make a version with a similar explosion of tropical flavors but that appeared more "classy," or something that you could easily sip at a proper cocktail party vs. a beach-side cabana. Meet the Classy Zombie. I kept that infamous three-rum base but instead of adding various citrus elements, I made a Grapefruit Oleo-Saccharum (page 165), an old school sweetener made from dissolving sugar in citrus oils. Then, instead of incorporating a spice element directly into the drink itself, I garnished with a smoldering piece of cinnamon, which always evokes tropical vibes.

¾ oz (22 ml) Jamaican rum

¾ oz (22 ml) Puerto Rican rum

½ oz (15 ml) 151-proof demerara rum

¼ oz (8 ml) Grapefruit Oleo-Saccharum (page 165)

1 tsp Grenadine (page 166)

2 dashes aromatic bitters

Herbsaint or absinthe rinse

Garnish: charred cinnamon stick

Combine the rums, Grapefruit Oleo-Saccharum, Grenadine and bitters in a mixing vessel with ice. Stir until chilled. Take a small spray bottle and lightly mist a rocks glass with Herbsaint. Place a large ice cube in the glass, and then strain your cocktail over it. Serve the cocktail on a coaster, alongside a charred cinnamon stick.

THE BARTENDER SUGGESTS
Smith & Cross Jamaican Pot Still Rum
Herbsaint Original 100 Proof
Hamilton 151 Overproof Demerara Rum

SYRUPS & INFUSIONS

SYRUPS

Sugar and sugar syrup does a lot more than just add sweetness to a drink. Sugar is an essential building block in many cocktails that helps provide both balance and texture (like using butter when baking). In addition to what I'd consider your "standard issue" cocktail syrups, such as Simple Syrup (page 160) and Demerara Syrup (page 160), you can also create various flavored or infused syrups to easily introduce another flavor element in your drinks.

TIPS FOR MAKING HOMEMADE COCKTAIL SYRUPS

- Simple syrups are equal parts water and sugar and it's recommended that you measure these parts by weight using a kitchen scale, instead of measuring by volume. This provides more accuracy.

- Use two parts sugar to one part water to make a Rich Simple Syrup, which is often used in spirit-forward cocktails. Its thicker texture adds additional sweetness without diluting a drink.

- Some syrups require heating in a pan on the stovetop to dissolve thicker sugars, or to help infuse certain ingredients. Always heat on the lowest setting necessary to dissolve the sugar and do not boil unless the specific syrup recipe says otherwise. Generally, if you boil your syrups, this will cause the water to evaporate and could quickly change the ratio and consistency of the syrup you're making.

- Keep cocktail syrups stored in resealable containers in the refrigerator. Mason jars or small glass bottles work great for this. If possible, date the syrup bottles when you make them, and if you haven't used them up in the following 2 to 3 weeks, you should throw them out. If left for too long, sugar syrup will develop mold and that's the last thing you want in your cocktails! Syrups that are made with fresh fruit tend to go bad or at least change in flavor faster.

- Fortify your cocktail syrups by adding a small amount of vodka to help extend the shelf life. There isn't necessarily a precise recommended amount, but just add a few drops or up to a teaspoon of vodka and shake the syrup container well.

SIMPLE SYRUP

This is your tried-and-true cocktail syrup that can be used in the majority of cocktails. If you're making a lot of cocktails, make Simple Syrup regularly and keep it stocked. However, it's also incredibly easy and quick to mix up a batch whenever you need it.

1 part sugar

1 part water

Combine the sugar and water in a resealable container. Shake or stir vigorously until the sugar is dissolved, or heat on low on the stove to help dissolve the sugar faster. Store in the refrigerator for up to 2 weeks.

NOTE: To make Rich Simple Syrup, use 2 parts sugar to 1 part water.

DEMERARA SYRUP

While not as universal as Simple Syrup, Demerara Syrup is the second syrup I believe everyone should keep ready-made. It's made with a richer, darker sugar with larger granules, similar to Sugar In The Raw®. It pairs especially well with aged spirits and adds a nice texture to more spirit-forward cocktails

2 parts demerara sugar

1 part water

Combine the sugar and water in a saucepan, and heat on low. Heat and stir just until the sugar is dissolved. Let the syrup cool, and then store in the refrigerator for up to 2 weeks.

HONEY OR AGAVE SIMPLE SYRUP

Both honey and agave nectar are fantastic cocktail sweeteners. However, both of these ingredients are naturally very sweet on their own, so use them sparingly. You may be tempted to just add them directly into your cocktail shaker or mixing glass, but neither substance mixes well on their own, especially when cold, so it's best to dilute them slightly into a syrup.

1 part honey or agave nectar

1 part water

Combine the honey or agave and water in a saucepan and heat on low. Heat and stir until the honey or agave is dissolved and fully combined into the water (try not to boil). Let the syrup cool, and then store in the refrigerator for up to 2 weeks.

SPICED SIMPLE SYRUP

This infused syrup is perfect for fall and winter cocktails. I like using the five specific spices listed below, but feel free to improvise here and use more, less or different spices that you prefer.

1 part sugar

1 part water

Whole cinnamon sticks

Whole cloves

Whole star anise

Crushed allspice

Fresh-cut ginger

Combine the sugar and water in a saucepan and heat on low heat. Stir until the sugar is fully dissolved. Add the spices to the saucepan. After 2 minutes, remove the syrup from the heat and allow the spices to steep in the syrup until it cools. To start, just use a small pinch of crushed allspice, 7 to 8 whole cloves and a 2-inch (5-cm) piece of fresh ginger, because these ingredients can go a long way. Both cinnamon and star anise are a little more forgiving, but start with 4 to 5 pieces of each. Strain out the solids, and then store in the refrigerator for up to 2 weeks.

NOTE: Try making this syrup with unsweetened cranberry juice instead of water (substituting equal parts) for a Spiced Cranberry Syrup that is ideal for holiday drinks like the Spiced Cranberry Sazerac (page 63).

JALAPEÑO AGAVE SYRUP

Want an easy way to spice up your Margaritas (page 39)—or nearly any cocktail for that matter? Jalapeño-Infused Syrup is the way to go. I use agave nectar as the sweetener base, but you can just as easily use regular sugar.

1 part agave nectar

1 part water

4–5 fresh jalapeño slices

Combine equal parts of agave nectar and water in a saucepan, and heat on low. Stir until the agave nectar and water are combined. Add the jalapeño slices. You can add as many as you like, adjusting for a more or less spicy syrup. Allow the jalapeño slices to steep in the syrup until it cools then store in the refrigerator for up to 2 weeks.

RASPBERRY SYRUP

BY JULIE REINER

Using fresh fruit to make cocktail syrups is a great way to incorporate those flavors into drinks without the mess of muddling. Yes, muddling fruit in a drink is faster but you're often left with solids that muck up your drink strainers. This is my preferred method.

½ cup (62 g) fresh raspberries (also works well with strawberries)

1 cup (200 g) granulated sugar

½ cup (120 ml) water

Smash up the raspberries and thoroughly mix with the sugar. Let the syrup sit for at least 30 minutes. Lightly heat the water (not boiling) and pour it over the mixture. Stir until all the sugar is dissolved. Strain through a sieve. Store in the fridge for around 2 weeks.

SPICY GINGER SYRUP

There's nothing quite like that fresh ginger zing! Once again, you could muddle a slice of freshly cut ginger in a cocktail, but taking a bit of extra time to make a syrup using ginger juice yields much better results. If you have a juicer, make a bit of fresh ginger juice; otherwise, many natural grocers have bottles of ginger juice in their produce section.

1 part granulated sugar

1 part ginger juice (fresh is best)

Combine equal parts sugar and ginger juice in a resealable container. Shake or stir until all the sugar is thoroughly dissolved. Store in the fridge for 1 to 2 weeks. Note that the fresh ginger spice does start to dull after just a few days.

VANILLA BEAN SYRUP

Vanilla Bean Syrup is a subtle upgrade to nearly any cocktail (try it in a classic Daiquiri [page 27]). The recipe involves using a whole vanilla bean pod, which you can remove after infusing, but I recommend leaving it in the syrup bottle while storing it in the fridge to keep that vanilla flavor nice and strong.

1 cup (200 g) granulated sugar

1 cup (240 ml) water

1 whole vanilla bean pod

Combine the sugar and water in a saucepan and heat on low. Cut a whole vanilla bean pod in half lengthwise, and carefully use your knife to scrape out the vanilla bean seeds. Place the pod and seeds in the syrup and stir until the sugar is dissolved. Let the syrup cool, and then pour it into a resealable container. Store in the fridge for 2 to 3 weeks.

RED WINE SYRUP

Creating syrups from wine and beer is another incredibly fun way to add new dynamics to your cocktails. You can simply add your desired wine or beer to a pan, heat them and make a reduction that can be used in place of a syrup. However, depending on the base ingredient, these reductions might not have enough sweetness to balance the cocktail you're making, so you can use wine or beer with equal parts sugar like in this recipe.

1 part organic cane sugar

1 part red wine

Combine the cane sugar and red wine in a saucepan, and heat on low. Stir until the sugar and wine are combined and the sugar dissolves, and then immediately remove the saucepan from the heat. Let the syrup cool, and then store it in the refrigerator for up to 2 weeks.

FRESH WATERMELON SYRUP

This syrup is guaranteed to brighten up any summer cocktail. As with most syrups made with fresh fruit, making this syrup fresh is best and the flavor will start to change or slightly dull after a few days. Definitely give this a try in a Margarita (page 39)!

1 small watermelon

1 part organic cane sugar (see instructions for measurement)

Cut a small watermelon into cubes and add the cubes to a blender and blend until smooth. Strain the juice through a fine mesh strainer and a coffee filter that has been saturated with water (ideally, the liquid will be clear, with no pulp). Use a kitchen scale to weigh the watermelon juice, and then use equal parts cane sugar of that weight and combine both in a saucepan on the stovetop. Heat on low and stir until combined. Let the syrup cool, and then store in the refrigerator for up to 1 week.

PINEAPPLE DEMERARA SYRUP

Making this syrup is almost like a fun little science experiment. It does not require heating or blending, but it does require some patience. Basically, just combine everything, let it sit for a few hours and you'll have a mind-blowing fresh-fruity syrup, as the sugar will draw out the juice and oils from the fruit and dissolve naturally. It's also a great way to make good use out of your pineapple scraps.

Scraps from 1 medium pineapple

3 whole limes

4–5 oz (112–140 grams) demerara sugar

Cut up a medium pineapple and put all the scraps (including the core) in a bowl. Enjoy the fruit however you'd like. Peel all three limes and add the peels to the pineapple scraps. Cover with demerara sugar and stir until all the fruit scraps are covered in sugar. Cover and let sit for 4 to 8 hours at room temperature, stirring occasionally to agitate the sugar. Once the sugar is dissolved, strain out the solids then store in the refrigerator for 1 to 2 weeks.

GRAPEFRUIT OLEO-SACCHARUM

Oleo-saccharum is an old school method of creating a citrusy sweetener for punches and early forms of cocktails without adding much dilution. It's an easy and interesting process that involves macerating citrus peels with sugar, drawing out the concentrated flavors from the fruit. I like using a mix of grapefruit and lemon peels, but try it out with orange peels or even peels of lime as well.

1½ cups (144 g) grapefruit and lemon peels

1 cup (200 g) organic cane sugar

Peel your citrus, avoiding the white pith as much as possible. Add the citrus peels and sugar to a bowl and stir to combine. You want the citrus peels to be thoroughly coated in sugar. Cover and let sit for 8 to 10 hours at room temperature, stirring occasionally to agitate the sugar. Once the sugar is dissolved, strain out the solids, and then store in the refrigerator for 1 to 2 weeks.

GRENADINE

This classic cocktail sweetener is super easy to make at home and is almost always guaranteed to be so much better than the artificial neon red grenadine you can buy at the store. While it has fallen out of fashion in recent years, this pomegranate-based sweetener is excellent in both cocktails and mocktails.

1 cup (240 ml) pomegranate juice

1 cup (200 g) cane sugar

Combine pomegranate juice and sugar in a pan on the stovetop. Heat on low while stirring, just until the sugar is dissolved into the pomegranate juice (do not boil). Once dissolved, immediately remove the pan from the heat. Let the syrup cool, and then store in the refrigerator for up to 3 weeks.

ORGEAT

This almond-based sweetener with a hard-to-pronounce French name is a key ingredient in many famous tropical cocktails, like the Mai Tai (page 142). It takes a bit of dedication to make, but it's well worth the effort. There are several other variations of Orgeat that are made with pumpkin seeds or avocado pits instead of almonds, so get wild with it if you want!

2 cups (286 g) blanched almonds

1½ cups (300 g) granulated sugar

1 cup (240 ml) water

1 oz (30 ml) brandy

½ tsp orange flower water

Pulse blanched almonds in a food processor until they are finely ground. Then, combine granulated sugar and water in a saucepan and heat on low. Stir until the sugar is dissolved, and then add the ground almonds. Allow to simmer for a few minutes, and then gradually increase the heat. Remove the pan just before boiling and cover it with a lid. Allow the mix to steep for at least 4 to 5 hours, and then strain through two layers of cheesecloth. Take the strained liquid and add brandy and orange flower water. Store in the fridge for 2 to 3 weeks.

Recommended Syrup Brands

There are syrups that I often use for cocktails that are either too time-consuming to make myself or require ingredients that are difficult to source in my region. Several that come to mind (and that I use in this book) are falernum and passion fruit syrup.

Falernum is a cocktail sweetener from the Caribbean, which has some similarities to Orgeat but with some added spices. In can also be made as a liqueur, using brandy or rum as the base. It can be fun to make your own, but since I use it often, I find it easier to purchase premade bottles from a reputable brand. Although I provided a recipe for Orgeat, this is another syrup I will often buy rather than make simply because I don't always have the time. Both passion fruit and guava syrup aren't that difficult to make but only rarely am I able to source these tropical fruits in my region.

For these types of time-consuming or more "exotic" ingredients, here are some quality brands that I personally recommend:

- **BG Reynolds:** This is my go-to company for all manner of tropical syrups and less-mainstream ingredients like a gardenia mix.

- **Small Hand Foods:** A small brand that is bartender-owned and operated. They have a small selection of syrups, but every single one is truly exceptional.

- **RAFT Syrups:** One of my favorite Portland-local brands that makes both bitters and quality cocktail syrups with unique flavors like smoked tea vanilla and pineapple tamarind.

- **Portland Syrups:** Another favorite Portland brand with a wide selection of syrup flavors that are geared toward using in both mocktails and cocktails. They make an amazing root beer syrup that is used in the Viking Colada (page 153).

- **Liber & Co.:** A fantastic small business that places the utmost importance on sourcing quality ingredients. Liber & Co. has a great selection of syrups, tonics and cordials.

INFUSIONS

Like cocktail syrups, you can also infuse spirits to incorporate other flavor elements into cocktails. This is usually done by combining a spirit with a solid ingredient and letting it sit at room temperature until the spirit absorbs some of the flavor and color of that ingredient before straining out the solids. You generally do not want to heat spirit infusions like you would cocktail syrups because any form of heat will cause the alcohol in the spirit to start evaporating.

Infusing spirits involves a bit of experimentation. The ratio of spirits to solid ingredients will vary on what you're infusing, and make sure you consider the total infusion time. Clear, unaged spirits like gin and vodka tend to draw out and absorb flavors faster than aged spirits do, so taste your infusion every so often and remove the solids whenever you feel like it's ready. If you're just starting out, I recommend only infusing a small amount of spirit in a mason jar vs infusing an entire bottle of liquor. Sometimes infusions don't go as planned or go horribly wrong, and you don't want to waste an entire bottle of precious spirit on a failed experiment.

HIBISCUS-INFUSED GIN

This infusion is the perfect way to introduce a bright red-pink color to your gin cocktails, as well as layering in a floral flavor element. I use dried hibiscus flowers, but using hibiscus tea also works well. The Runway Magic cocktail (page 48) calls for Hibiscus-Infused Gin but also consider trying this infusion with vodka or tequila blanco.

2 heaping tbsp (6 g) dried hibiscus flowers or hibiscus tea

2 cups (480 ml) gin

Combine dried hibiscus flowers (or hibiscus tea) with gin or your clear spirit of choice. Mix in a mason jar, seal it and shake every couple hours. Let it infuse for around 24 hours, tasting every few hours until you're happy with the overall flavor. Strain through a fine mesh strainer and discard the flowers. Store in a resealable container in a cool, dark place.

BUTTERFLY PEA BLOSSOM— INFUSED MEZCAL

This infusion is strictly for the striking blue color. Once infused, butterfly pea blossom creates a natural indigo hue that changes colors when the pH level of the drink changes (i.e., adding something like citrus juice). It has little to no perceivable flavor of its own and is really used for creating a beautiful aesthetic.

1 tbsp (3 g) dried butterfly pea flowers

2 cups (480 ml) mezcal

Combine the butterfly pea flowers and mezcal in a mason jar, seal it and gently shake. Let it sit until the spirit is a dark blue color (usually only takes 20 to 30 minutes). Strain through a fine mesh strainer and discard the flowers. Store in a resealable container in a cool, dark place.

CACAO NIB—INFUSED TEQUILA AÑEJO

Roasted cacao nibs can add an incredibly rich and decadent layer to aged spirits. I love how this infusion seems to automatically make cocktails taste more like a dessert without adding any sugar. The Nocturnal Burn (page 72) features this infusion using an aged tequila, but try it out with your favorite whiskey or aged rum as well.

2 tbsp (15 g) roasted cacao nibs

2 cups (480 ml) tequila añejo

Combine the cacao nibs and tequila in a mason jar and infuse for 1 to 2 days, shaking occasionally to agitate the ingredients. Taste the infusion every so often until you're happy with the overall flavor. Strain out the solids and store the infusion in a resealable container in a cool, dark place.

BROWN BUTTER-WASHED VODKA

"Fat washing" is a fun method for infusing spirits with various oils and fats. These types of infusions usually result in subtle flavors and aromas, but often drastically change the texture or mouthfeel of a spirit. Although I don't use vodka often, a neutral spirit is a great choice when you really want the subtilties of an infusion to come through.

4 tbsp (57 g) butter

2 cups (480 ml) vodka

Brown the butter in a saucepan by heating the butter over low heat and constantly stirring. You'll notice the butter gradually turning brown in appearance and there will be a delicious nutty aroma when it's ready. Be careful not to burn it, as it can go from brown to burnt very quickly. Remove the browned butter from the heat and allow it to cool slightly, but not enough to re-solidify. Pour it into a jar, and then add the vodka and screw on the lid. Let it sit for an hour or two, shaking the jar on occasion. Then, place it in the freezer for several hours until all the butter is frozen solid. It typically forms a thin layer or "puck" on the surface. Puncture a hole in the frozen layer and pour out the infused vodka into a clean container. You may need to strain the vodka through cheesecloth or a coffee filter to remove all the butter solids. Store the infused vodka in a resealable container in a cool, dark place.

ACKNOWLEDGMENTS

First and foremost, thank you to my wonderful wife Ellie for supporting me throughout my life and career, and especially while writing this book. It's because of your encouragement, support and patience that I am in the position I am today. I love you more than I can say.

Thank you to my wonderful parents, David and Vickie, for loving and supporting me no matter what. I've always so deeply appreciated the way you both show genuine interest in what I do even though you aren't big fans of cocktails or alcohol. I've never once doubted that you are both in my corner. I hope I'll be as good a parent someday as you both are to me.

Thank you to professional bartender friends, authors and icons who I've always looked up to; namely Jeffrey Morgenthaler, Ryan Magarian and Jim Meehan.

Thank you to friends like Tara Fougner of Thirsty Media, Emily Arden Wells of Gastronomista and Elliott Clark of Apartment Bartender. Each of you were, and are, big inspirations for me, and I am forever grateful for all that you've done to help me succeed. Thank you as well to my designers, Small Caps Co..

Thank you to good friends and fellow cocktail creators Miguel Buencamino, Barlow Gilmore, Jason Plummer and Justin Alford. I love having all of you guys just one group-text away. Here's to more boozy adventures together soon!

Thank you to the amazing friends and bartenders who contributed recipes for this book, namely Jeffrey Morgenthaler, Lydia McLuen, Ricky Gomez, Jessica Braasch, Ryan Magarian and Danijela Leknaviciute.

Thank you to my old friend Ian Pratt for making me my first ever Old Fashioned. All of this is your fault!

Thank you to my friends at PDX Ice, who supplied me when photographing this book.

Thank you to all my bartender friends and acquaintances in Portland, Seattle, Los Angles, New York, New Orleans and beyond for welcoming me into this industry and helping me do what I do. You are the reason the hospitality industry is so beautiful and vibrant.

Of course, thank you so much to my publisher Page Street Publishing Co. and to Franny Donington for reaching out to me and working closely with me to make this book a reality. Writing a book was on my bucket list, but I had no idea how to make it happen. Thank you for making this such a fun and smooth process, and for working so collaboratively with me.

ABOUT THE AUTHOR

JORDAN HUGHES is a full-time creative in the food & beverage industry. He works as a photographer, recipe developer and media consultant for respected brands, bars and restaurant groups. In 2017, he started the Instagram and blog High-Proof Preacher, which has since been featured in *Forbes*, AskMen, Liquor.com and VinePair, and was awarded both the editor's and reader's choice for Best Drinks Instagram 2019 by *Saveur* magazine.

More recently, Jordan has entered the e-learning space, launching a digital learning platform called Cocktail Camera that aims to help aspiring photographers, as well as bartenders, expand on their skills by learning to better capture beverages and products.

Jordan currently lives in Portland, Oregon, where he was born and raised. In addition to making cocktails and taking photos, he enjoys spending as much time as possible with his wife Ellie and their family. Be sure to find him on various social media platforms and follow along at @highproofpreacher and @cocktailcamera.

INDEX